"Everyone who has lived had a history and each life impacts the life of another either positively or negatively. Some life histories even impact the future lives of thousands. But, even fewer significant life histories impact the eternal lives of others. This life story will impact yours forever!"

—Roger Bourgeois
Pastor
Fellowship of Living Praise
Clermont, GA
www.fellowshipoflivingpraise.org

"Holly Payne has overcome what most people would consider to be insurmountable odds. If you have a loved one with an 'I can't' attitude, be sure to give them a copy of *Fire on Wheels*. It's physical proof that we can do all things through Christ who strengthens us."

—Scott Cooper
Founder and Director
Scott Cooper Ministries
www.edgeoftheriver.org

"*Wow!* I was totally in awe when I read this book. It was truly an inspiration by the Holy Spirit. Through knowing Holly and reading this incredible book I now have hope and hope for everyone who needs prayer."

—Dee Anderson
Apostolic Ambassador
The Father's Gateway Ministry
Sautee, Georgia
www.thefathersgateway.com

"Holly is one of my closest heart friends. I have seen the rarest side of God through her. I honor her and cherish her heart of love for God and mankind. God has brought her into our world for a specific purpose not just to be a beacon of light for a dark world but a beacon of Hope for all. I am astounded at her insights into the many facets of God.

This book is a hard one to put down or skip a sentence. I encourage you beloved reader, to get ready to be rewarded with some 'mind-blowing, hair blown back' truths, embrace them to your delight like I did. We shall then be a beacon of Hope like Holly is!!"

—"Shanti"
Iris India
www.irisindia1040.com

"*Fire on Wheels* brings home the importance of having an intimate relationship with God the Father and the power of knowing who you are in Christ."

—Chuck Huskins
Director, Reconcile to God Ministries

"*Fire on Wheels* is a picture drawn with words describing a woman who refuses to let her physical limitations define her life. She may be physically confined in a wheel chair, but she walks in more freedom and obedience to the call of God on her life than most of us who are without excuse. *Fire on Wheels* will leave its readers a desire to live with passion and fire!"

—Sandy Starnes,
Christ Fellowship

"Holly Payne is without question the most courageous person I know. There is always a smile on her face and she is the first one to step forward to offer help when a need arises. It is only natural for the joy that flows from Holly's heart to flow when she puts pen to paper. This book is full of joy, unspeakable joy, wisdom, and encouragement. The reader will definitely get a new flame for his or her heels (or wheels)."

—Maxie L. Hellmann
Chaplain, Author

Fire on Wheels

Fire on Wheels
'til I'm Fire on Heels

HOLLY PAYNE

TATE PUBLISHING
AND ENTERPRISES, LLC

Published by Tate Publishing & Enterprises, LLC
127 E. Trade Center Terrace | Mustang, Oklahoma 73064 USA
1.888.361.9473 | www.tatepublishing.com

Tate Publishing is committed to excellence in the publishing industry. The company reflects the philosophy established by the founders, based on Psalm 68:11,
"The Lord gave the word and great was the company of those who published it."

Book design copyright © 2014 by Tate Publishing, LLC. All rights reserved.
Cover design by Jim Villaflores
Interior design by Gram Telen

Published in the United States of America

ISBN: 978-1-63268-057-0
1. Religion / Christian Life / Spiritual Growth
2. Religion / Christian Life / Professional Growth
14.04.23

Dedication

This book is dedicated to Jesus and his Kingdom.
Maranatha!

Acknowledgments

There are so many people in my life for whom I'm thankful. All of them have in some way contributed to the process which culminated with this book. So to everyone who has taken part in the story of my life, I extend my heartfelt gratitude.

To Mom, a pillar of strength for so many, thank you. It has to be God who has given you the strength and fortitude to carry the responsibilities that you have. I'm eternally grateful to be able to call you Mom and my friend.

To Sissy, who is always "my buddy." Simply put, you're beautiful and I love you.

To Ken, Teresa, Brittany, and Patrick, thank you for loving God and encouraging me in my pursuit of him. To Conner and Chloe, my "Boogie" and "Shoogie," you make me laugh and warm my heart!

To my friends, who are also my family by the Blood of Jesus, I am thankful beyond measure for your support and thoughtfulness. You've seen the kingdom potential in me and dared me to dream. Then you've accepted those dreams as an already-established fact. There are too many of you to list here, but from right here in my own north Georgia region, to southern Georgia, to Ohio, to South Carolina, to India, and everywhere in between, I know who you are, and I know that you know who you are.

To everyone on the council of Deep Calls to Deep Ministries, you are fantastic and I am thankful to you.

To my church family, thank you for staying the course and giving me a safe and strong place to grow.

To the International Institute of Mentoring and all of the incredible people I've met there and through there, I'm grateful for your persistent encouragement.

And finally, to Daddy, who I still miss but who is now cheering me on from heaven, thank you for the foundation of faith. I promise to build on it wisely.

I love each and every one of you.

Contents

Foreword

If I were to describe anyone as "fire on wheels" it would definitely be Miss Holly Payne! She is one of the most tenacious women that I have ever known. Her determination and drive to impact the world with the message of Christ is unwavering, even in the midst of what some would see as personal challenges.

I first came to know Holly as a mentee in the International Institute of Mentoring, and I instantly witnessed her sincere passion to reach the lost and hurting with the message of wholeness through healing in Christ. She quickly excelled in our mentoring program and won the hearts of her peers and mentors. Holly has many talents that others may not recognize immediately, as she is quite humble about her expertise in technology, education, and ministry. However, the spiritual insight that she shares in this book is undeniable.

In her book, *Fire on Wheels til' I'm Fire on Heels*, Holly provides you with the encouragement and evidence that no obstacle is too great to be conquered for your calling. In her warm and witty way, Holly shares her own personal journey of discovering contentment in any challenge and embracing wholeness in any season. Holly is proof that no matter what you face, you can be an overcomer! The power of forgiveness, healing, authenticity and grace is so beautifully displayed in Holly's life, and I know that this book will ignite the same fire in you to chase after every promise God has for you.

Pastor Judy Jacobs Tuttle
Evangelist, Author & Co-Pastor of
Dwelling Place Church International

Introduction

Every life on earth has a kingdom purpose. There are no happenstances. It's all intentional on someone's part and none of it is lost in the mix. That's what I love about it. Every little detail matters, not just the big ones. It's the little details that add up to make the bigger picture.

Over the last few years, I've had people ask me repeatedly if I've written a book about my life and the lessons I've learned. It had been something I'd considered, but every time I had started it, the project would just stall out, for lack of a better way to explain it. Then finally, I realized why. In part, it is because I have always been far more interested in living life than in writing about it. I was just too busy. Those who know me well know how much I love to be on the move sitting still only when absolutely necessary. Just because I sit doesn't mean I have to sit still! But the delay was really deeper than that. It meant opening up the rooms in the deepest parts of who I am to examine them in the fullness of the *light* of Jesus. Were those places healed? Could I bear sharing them? Could I bear looking at them myself? For all the previous times I'd considered sharing my story, the answer had been no. Until now, I wasn't ready.

Then, not long ago, the Lord began speaking to my heart about finally writing such a book. At first, I thought the same old thoughts and asked him the same old questions like, "Lord, what is my life that people would want to read about it anyway? What do I have to say that would impact others?"

In no uncertain terms, he reminded me how mindful of my life he has been; how he has kept me even when I didn't make it easy to be kept; and how he has really given me a remarkable testimony. He's spoken to me often about how our testimonies coupled with the *blood* of Christ are how we overcome. The *blood* of Christ is what saves and sets us free, but our testimonies are testaments to others of his faithfulness to empower us for ongoing victory beyond our initial experiences of his love. That's when I realized that it was time to write it. It was time to share what he's done in my life as a means of glorifying him, and it was just a logical part of the lifelong process of overcoming.

I've prayed about what parts of my own story to include in this book, and have proceeded as he's led with sharing those, as well as the lessons learned during my walk of faith. I've been led to share some details and personal stories, but not all are necessarily in chronological order. Each personal story that I've shared includes some specific lesson, and sometimes more than one. For me, the entire purpose of sharing with you is the hope that it will draw you closer to the Lord. So each of the lessons I've shared is one I've personally learned and has drawn me closer into a place of intimacy with him. For me, that's what it always comes down to. It's a relationship with a real being, an infinite Creator who is also a very personal friend and Father. I love sharing him…not just sharing *about* him, but sharing *him*. That means I love *truth*, even the parts that remind me of all the things that are sure proof I am human and have made some major mistakes. Those are the things that have made grace the most real to me. I used to think I could only talk about or share from the experiences I've had directly. Then I realized that was a subtle lie of the enemy. To do so would be limiting my story to only experiential knowledge of Jesus.

When I was about nineteen and getting ready to graduate from the first college I attended, I really began pressing into him to discover his purpose for me. It didn't take long for me to realize I could never be completely happy unless I was serving him with my life. When I asked him what I should focus on being able to share, he said something that shocked me.

"Healing and deliverance."

I sat there and thought, "Lord, *what?*"

"You heard me right."

I thought it was profoundly amusing that of all topics, he'd want me to be acquainted with healing and deliverance. He gently reminded me that his foolishness is wiser than man's wisdom and that his weakness is stronger than man's strength. In 1 Corinthians 1:27 (NASB), he tells us that he "has chosen the foolish things of the world to shame the wise, and…the weak things to shame the things which are strong."

So I began to study and soak in all of what he placed in my path. I developed a voracious appetite for knowing him as the Lord of liberty. Over time, I became utterly convinced that healing *is* the children's bread, and I live in expectation of it. At the time of this writing, I am still seated and have not experienced the miracle that makes me able to walk. The enemy of my soul would love to use that to disqualify me from speaking of my king's miraculous healing power and all his benefits. If I were relying on my adequacy alone, he'd be right. *But God* has made a way by allowing us to claim for ourselves things based on the adequacy which comes from him and not from ourselves.

> Such confidence we have through Christ toward God. Not that we are adequate in ourselves to consider anything as *coming* from ourselves, but our adequacy is from God, who also made us adequate as servants of a new covenant, not of the letter but of the Spirit; for the letter kills, but the Spirit gives life.
>
> 2 Corinthians 3:4–6 (NASB)

So the enemy has no grounds for his argument. God's word has declared it null and void. I do not have to rely on only my own experiences, but rather on the word of the Lord and all of the promises contained in it, whether I've personally experienced them yet or not. That's where real faith steps in. It's at that point where we boldly decide to declare those things that are not as though they were. I've come to believe that they *are* whether we see them or not. That's a basic principle of faith. We accept and believe in a God we can't physically see. So it's the same when we preach a principle of faith even before we see it manifest personally. Besides, in addition to physical healing, there are many other types of healing, including emotional and spiritual. I have most definitely experienced his touch of healing in those areas. The Gospel, or "good news," is the Gospel in entirety, so if one part is true, then by faith, we must accept the rest as true. When we speak of his Gospel, we can't just conveniently leave out the parts we haven't quite figured out yet. We declare the good news as *truth* from the competency of his word, not from our experiences of his word.

Holy Spirit has also been quick to remind me that our testimonies never end. Some people think "testimony" is equivalent to "salvation experience." But it isn't. Our testimonies begin the moment we do (which is at conception, not birth, by the way) and they do not end when we take our last breaths. I am firmly convinced that our testimonies continue into eternity and encompass all of our existence in his direct presence. So this book is really "my life and adventures, thus far" and only a snapshot of things and lessons learned at this point. I'm fully anticipatory of many more experiences and lessons. Only God possesses the book of my life in which he has recorded everything about me from before I began (Psalm 139:16).

So...

Hey, there. My name is Holly, but I'm also "fire on wheels"!

Getting Comfortable in My Own Skin

Our self-image is an interesting tool. It can make or break us, but the truth is that it should never become a stronghold. For many though, it does. While a lot of people tend to think this is only an issue for teen girls and women, that's not true. If men are honest, they will admit that their self-image is very important. I can't explain the pure shock I experienced when I realized that some of my male friends are every bit as vain as me or any of my female friends! If I'm going to be totally honest, there was a good bit of relief in discovering that.

When I was a young child, I really looked no different than most. As a baby, I had white blonde hair and super-blue eyes. All throughout my infancy and toddlerhood, I was one of the most well-dressed little girls around. My dad worked at a factory called Warren Featherbone Co., which was a babies' and children's clothing manufacturer. The factory shipped clothing to lots of major department stores, but it also had a sales room where the local public could come and buy the clothes. On a regular basis, the displays would be rotated and have new styles brought in. Because of my age, I was a prime target to receive all the sample display items as they came down. I had all kinds of dresses and outfits that my dad was proud to get to bring home, and my mom was proud to get to dress me in.

Of course I was too young to remember most of that, but people tell me that I rarely wore the same outfit twice. But at a young age, I grew accustomed to people talking about what a cute little girl I was. By the time I was four years old, my golden hair was down almost to my rump and I loved my frills. My brother, Ken, had a snazzy sunflower yellow Corvette convertible, so he'd take me places with him too. For such a young child, riding in my big brother's car was better than an amusement park ride. According to family anecdotes, I was as precocious as they come. But also during this toddlerhood season of my life, other things were happening.

When I was about nine months old, my parents first started realizing that when I was sitting up, I seemed "floppy," with a tendency to droop to one side. Upon closer inspection, they saw what appeared to be a curvature in my spine. They also realized I was not progressing with my motor skills like other babies my age. When it came to intelligence and cognition, I was advanced. To this day, my family teases me and says that I was born talking and that I've never met a stranger. But back in those days, as most parents would have been, they were concerned about the lack of physical strength development. At first, doctors just believed I was a late bloomer and said not to worry, but when I had passed a year of age and still wasn't able to crawl forward or pull up and walk, even doctors decided it was time to test me for some answers.

My mother, brother, and sister at my first birthday, just before the diagnosis.

At the age of fifteen months, I was admitted into a high profile children's hospital in Atlanta for an extensive battery of tests. There, doctors confirmed that I was advanced in development in regard to mental abilities, but after several other tests, including a muscle biopsy that left me with a scar I still carry, they had what they believed was the most accurate diagnosis. In those days, they called it "Werdnig-Hoffman disease" or "infantile progressive spinal muscular atrophy." The overall prognosis doctors gave was not good. I was given a projected life span of no more than three years. It was declared that I would have numerous bouts of pneumonia, and while the disease itself would not kill me, eventually the story went that I would succumb to respiratory failure due to lack of strength. In the meantime, they said I would never walk, or even stand, and would be bound to a wheelchair for the duration of my exceedingly short life. My parents were told to bring me home and love me for the little bit of time I had left. Needless to say, they were devastated.

When I had my follow-up visit with my local pediatrician, my mother tells me that he sat there and cried as he read the results. He had a disabled child himself, and he was well-acquainted with the difficult road we were just being told we were now on. Finally, he said the first promising thing she'd heard in a while.

"Take her home and love her, but treat her like any other child. We don't know everything."

He made no promises, but he also knew that he wasn't God. Neither was any other doctor. So he basically gave her an open-ended duration to my life.

As a result, I came home and my family chose to believe that I could live in spite of what doctors had said. Fifteen months turned into two years. Two years turned into three. Eventually, I was five and it was time to go to school. By this time, I had been using a manual wheelchair for three years. It was long before the Americans with Disabilities Act, so lots of areas were not physically accessible for wheelchair users, and my dad was initially very hesitant about sending me to school. In fact, early on, he adamantly opposed it. Eventually though, he realized it was something that needed to happen, so my mom enrolled me in school. That began a huge part of how I'd later define myself.

Up until then, I was still that cute little girl. My sister and brother were significantly older than me. Around the time I started school, I started gaining weight much more rapidly than most kids. I would eat the same foods and in the same amounts as my other friends and cousins, but when we'd all go back out to play, they were running and burning their calories off and I wasn't, since I was on wheels. I don't remember how old I was when I had a particular disconcerting experience, but I remember the experience itself clearly. I hadn't been in the practice of looking into mirrors regularly, but I remembered what I had looked like earlier, and I remembered what I looked like in previous pictures of myself, so I had assumed that's what I still looked like. Then one day I looked in a mirror. I didn't recognize myself. What I saw truly disappointed me, and I was still just a very young child. But at that moment, the enemy of my soul planted a seed of disappointment with my appearance. I saw a fat kid, and I knew what happened to fat kids. People made fun of them.

From that point on, I hated pictures of me. I dreaded picture day at school. I wanted to draw absolutely *no* attention to myself because I didn't want people to look at me. It became a huge issue with me. Although honestly, in retrospect, I seriously doubt anyone knew how I felt. It was so real to me though that it became truth to me.

In high school, I hit a really tough low in regards to appearance. If I'm being honest, I think I probably didn't feel like I had any worth whatsoever based on how I looked, so I developed a big case of what I call "I-don't-give-a-ripness." I was so involved in academics and extracurricular activities that I hoped it would take the focus off of how badly I felt about myself. I wore jeans, T-shirts, wacky print blouses and plaid flannel overshirts. I *wanted* to be keen on fashion and I definitely kept up with things by eagerly devouring *Teen Magazine* each month, but no one could have told it by looking at me. The only accessories I really collected and wore regularly were watches and rings, and I had so many that my family joked with me about the huge collection I had. At least I kept those stylish! Even a down-in-the-dumps chick knows bling makes everything better!

When I graduated from high school and went to college, it felt in some ways like a fresh start. With the new beginning and surrounded by many new people, I found myself digging back into my really girlie girl side. I rediscovered how much I had loved makeup and painted nails earlier in my life. I remembered how, as a little girl, everything had to have glitter or sparkles, from my school supplies to my shoes. I let my hair grow back out long and un-permed, and overall, I just decided that even if I was fat, I was going to do what I could with it.

I had accepted Christ about four years prior to that, and looking back, I realized that it was the love of Jesus healing my heart from the inside out that let me begin this external transformation process. Looking in mirrors still wasn't my favorite thing, and at times, I'd still cringe. There were even times when I'd cry. But over a period of years, I started noticing something. The more I fell in love with Jesus, the easier it was to look in a mirror.

It has been a slow process, and there are still days when I struggle with the image in the mirror even now, but I also now know it is as much a spiritual condition as it is a physical condition. While I can't physically do a lot of exercise (yet), I stay as active as I can. God's Word teaches us that our bodies are temples of the Holy Spirit. So for several years, I've been especially attentive to nutrition and the foods I put into my body.

Interestingly enough, as I've become more comfortable with myself, some weight has come off. It's far slower for me than for more active individuals, but it's at least progress and I'm grateful.

The most freedom in the area of accepting myself came when I realized what was happening when I *didn't* accept myself.

> Then God said, Let Us make man in Our image, according to Our likeness
>
> Genesis 1:26 (NASB)

I realized that our bodies are made in the very image of God. Do I mean that God is a fat human in a wheelchair? Of course not. But we are created in the general image of an Almighty Father who could have created us to look like anything. Can you imagine the thought of being made to look like an armadillo? Or a porcupine? Or an iguana? Praise God He made me in his image, not in an iguana's image! I don't think I could rock the spiked mohawk look. But kudos to those who can! Seriously though, Christ lives in us through the Holy Spirit and in the Father's very image. So when we reject ourselves, we are rejecting the very image of God on earth.

I had a heart change—an attitude adjustment. One of the greatest examples that led to this heart change came through an unexpected source.

I have an older sister and brother. My sister has Down's syndrome and, for me, is one of the most beautiful souls on earth. She's funny, loveable, and loving. There are no small things to her. Everything is a big deal. Many people might look at someone like her and describe her in many ways, but oftentimes, people with Down's are harshly called anything but beautiful.

My beautiful Sissy as a teenager

One day, I had just finished putting on my lipstick. I have this funky hot pink mirror with two ends on a bendable chrome frame. I've had it for years and though it's funky, it's still fun and functional. So on this particular day, I spun the mirror around so Sissy could see herself. I smiled and asked, "Who's that?" She looked into the mirror and grinned.

"That's me!" she declared proudly.

"And you're beautiful, right?" I asked.

"Yeah!" she said, grinning bigger and craning her neck to get a better view of her own reflection.

My heart bubbled over with warmth and love. She has no preconceived notions of what the world defines as beauty. She just sees her own face as a reflection that's beautiful. And that's awesome to me. In those moments that day, I sat and marveled about the innocent way she wholeheartedly accepted that she's beautiful. I pray that we would all learn from examples like that!

Sissy's simple message made me take a long look at my own views. She spoke volumes in only those few words. It was a huge challenge for me.

I made it even more of a point over the next couple of years just to *be*. Oh, I still wore my makeup, and I still do. As the silly old proverb goes, "Every old barn can use a fresh coat of paint!" Makeup and nails are fun for me, but those things no longer fuel my self-image. I just focused on allowing myself to be more open to the Holy Spirit's healing work in my life. As I did, something very interesting began happening.

"Holly, what's different about you? You look amazing."

"You're glowing…did you use a new makeup?"

"You are so beautiful. You always look so happy."

Then finally, someone pegged it.

"The Holy Spirit is just shining through you!"

Rarely in my life since that very early childhood time had people used such descriptions for me. I began feeling different. As I prayed one evening, I heard the Lord gently speak to my healing spirit.

"Choosing to be beautiful comes from the inside out."

Instantly, I realized that he meant we have to choose to let him do his work in us. It also meant that a lot of what we call brokenness really is nothing more than an unwillingness to let him do that work in us. True brokenness is a healing process devoid of pride, because we must acknowledge it before he can redeem it.

Self-hatred and self-loathing are tools of the enemy to make us focus on us instead of the Christ in us. It's a lie he uses to misguide and redirect us from the truth and from fulfilling our destinies. If he can get us to be so self-conscious that we hate our image so much and can't bear standing in front of others, whether before one other or before a stadium of thousands, he has effectively knocked us out of our position of authority. He has made the lie of inferiority so believable that we buy into it without seeing the complete acceptance we're giving up to receive inferiority in return. If my body in its current state is a place where the Holy Spirit himself is happy to dwell, then I am certainly honored to let him take up residence in me. I am more than willing to let him take me from glory to glory. It only gets better from the moment we take our focus off of our self-image and place it on our Christ-image. We are to boast in him and of his glory, and the only way we can do that is to make sure people see him in and through us.

I'm still not what a lot of the world calls beautiful. I still have extra weight that I'm working at getting off, and a lot of it to be frank, but it is for health and convenience reasons that I keep pressing toward that goal more than anything now. I've come to the conclusion that if someone doesn't like the way I look, that's their problem and not mine. That might sound arrogant, but it isn't because what I mean is that as long as I am making a conscious decision to let Christ shine through me, then it isn't me people are rejecting. It's Christ in me they're rejecting. That is between them and

God, not between them and me. And I'm fantastically okay with that.

Moments of Reflection

1. How do you release your own struggles with self-image?

2. In whose image are you made?

3. What are five things you like about yourself?

4. How do you like to pamper yourself?

5. Say something nice to compliment at least five people today. How do you see it impact them?

Prayer of Refining

Dear Abba, thank you for making me in your image. Reveal to me the areas of my life and self-image in which I have believed the lies of the enemy. I repent of believing those lies and I accept that your word toward me and in me is true. Lord, thank you for healing those areas and revealing the beauty of who I am in you. From this day forward, I declare and decree that I will see myself as you see me, that I will live my life as a reflection of your glory in me, and that I will take it even a step further by taking the time to see the reflection of your glory in others and telling them so.

In the name of Jesus, so be it. Amen!

Releasing the Roar Inside

My cousin, Eric, and I on a family vacation.

I've never liked confrontation, but inside, I've always been highly competitive. That seems like an oxymoron, but it is possible. It most likely began when I was in school. Since dealing with the symptoms of the spinal muscular atrophy diagnosis, I wasn't really able to participate in sports. My only real sporting adventures revolved around the makeshift baseball games my cousin Eric and I used to play in my front yard when we were kids. Oh, and the light saber duels we had, using old antenna prongs as our sabers, back when Star Wars was new on the scene and so popular. Quite honestly, if I had been able to, I'd probably have lived as much of my life as possible outside. To this day, I adore being outside as long as my fair skin isn't broiling. However, because sports-related activities were not an option for me, I found my niche in academics.

Even before I began school, it was obvious that I had an extreme interest in learning. I was able to write my name at fifteen months of age. It wasn't necessarily superbly penned, and it might take up an entire sheet of paper, but I was able to do it. When I was in kindergarten, one of my teachers spoke to my mother and told her I was very advanced and they really had nothing new to offer me. Even so, I loved school and had a lot of fun. By fifth grade, I was getting to skip my own spelling class so I could go to a second grade classroom and help tutor younger kids who were having problems with spelling. I loved reading, writing, and drawing. Every time there was a contest, I entered it, and often won.

Valedictory speech at my high school graduation

This pattern of pushing myself continued until I graduated as valedictorian in 1995. It wasn't really that I wanted to sail past other people. Instead, it was more that I wanted to push myself beyond each of my own previous achievements. Competitive, yes, but I was in competition with myself. I took great pride in these accomplishments. It was rewarding to know that I could place my efforts on something, work hard at it, and see it pay off. Sometimes the payoff was a ribbon. Other times it was a medal. At the end of public school and on into college, it came in the form of monetary rewards and scholarships.

I don't say any of this to brag about myself. I say it to describe the prison cell of pride I studied myself right into. From a worldly viewpoint, it seems like a very good thing. But it became a stronghold of pride. For me, doing well at academics meant I was actually good at something. I felt terrible about myself as a person and I didn't like my appearance. Most of all, I hated my own limitations. But when I was at school, excelling, for a while, everything felt right, even if it was temporary.

There were some glitches along the way though. There was the one high-profile man in my hometown who once voiced an opinion that kids with disabilities didn't even need to be in public school because they were "never going to be able to do anything anyway." There was the lady who specifically made snide and hurtful comments about me. And there was that person who said I only ever won anything because people felt sorry for me, and it wasn't fair to the other kids. Comments like these hurt me tremendously, and the enemy of our souls is a tricky thief and destroyer. He used those comments, and the many other similar ones, to chip away at the only area in life where I had any confidence whatsoever. They were all lies whispered into the hearts of individuals who gave them a voice. I've since dealt with the pain and scars of those statements by placing them at the feet of Jesus, but in their time and for years, they did hurt. But I was able to see the truth. I *had* worked hard. And standardized tests where I ranked in the 98th and 99th percentile nationwide didn't lie. Those scorers in another state didn't know anything about me, so they couldn't be just giving me scores because they felt bad for me. And the art contest judges, who looked at pieces that were numbered randomly without my name on them, had no clue whose work they were judging. I knew the truth, but the words and accusations were sharp and wounding.

My love for drawing started as a child,
but this is a more recent piece.

Confrontation in those days wasn't an option for me. I secretly wanted to tell people off, but I'd always been taught to respect my elders, so the only way I knew to right those wrongs was by working even harder to prove them all false. I didn't have the confidence to do anything except to stay in my element.

Throughout all my years of being on the student side of academics, I was a complete workaholic and overachiever. It paid off in the end, but to be honest, there were times when I am pretty sure I missed out on some of the fun because I was more focused on doing than on being. In fact, for me, all of my "being" was wrapped up in the identity of what I was "doing." It wasn't until years later, in my late twenties or early thirties, that I realized this condition had a name—performance orientation. It also wasn't really until then that I realized it had been a stronghold all of my life.

When I prayed to be set free from performance orientation, I began to notice lots of areas where it had taken root. By that point, I had been teaching for several years. People often told me how they wished they were as bold and confident as I was. I would thank them, but inside, I'd be thinking to myself, *If only they knew.* As I continued to take stock of where this appearance of boldness came from, I didn't like discovering that most of it was based on achievement. If I stripped away all the things I had done, I didn't feel like I had any worth at all, and that was a very uncomfortable state of realization.

It all became perfectly clear when I entered a second master's program. My mind was telling me it was a good, logical choice, but my heart wasn't in it. Looking back, I see clearly that the Lord never really led me to do it. It was just to try to achieve something else. But because my heart wasn't in it, I felt completely disconnected from the program, and I ended up taking an F in a class simply because I simply could not make myself "do" one more thing in a program to which my Father had not called me. The world didn't end when I got my grade report that semester. In an honest discussion with my department head at work the next Friday afternoon, I told him I was miserable in the program. With much grace, he told me he would never expect me to remain in a program I was miserable in. I felt a huge weight lift from me when I saw that he wasn't disappointed with me. What I had perceived as a personal failure dissolved right before my eyes.

I left his office and went to my office to e-mail my advisor and professor to tell him I was dropping out of the program. I felt instant relief, and I sensed in my spirit that something profound had just happened. As I rolled down the hall to the elevator that afternoon to go home, I knew I had turned a corner.

It was also at that precise time that I became acutely aware of my need for boldness beyond my own abilities to achieve. That's when I really studied about and began to seek the baptism of the Holy Spirit. It's kind of humorous in retrospect. It was a long time before I could receive the baptism because I was trying so hard to receive it. I was still attempting to use what I'd always used when I wanted to achieve something. I was falling right back into that old place of performance orientation. The thing I was seeking healing from in that season was the very thing I was attempting to use to obtain the healing.

"Forgive me for being so blunt, but you're trying too hard," a friend basically told me one night, though those might not have been his exact words.

At first, the comment rubbed me the wrong way... until I realized he was exactly right. So I stopped trying. I just spent time in worship and in reading the Bible, and soon after that, with myself out of the way, the baptism came, and with it came a new boldness I'd never experienced. Grace himself blew right through me, casting down the need to do anything in my own strength or abilities. I thought I had understood grace, but until then, I hadn't.

Over the next few years, I felt the chains and fetters falling away. I was tired of trying so hard to do well at things. It wasn't that I had become lazy, nor was it that I despised a spirit of excellence. Even now, I believe that if God calls us to do something and we accept the call, we *should* do it with a spirit of excellence. But the defining factor should be the unction from the Holy Spirit, and not from a place of needing to perform to prove self-worth and value. I had reached a place of wanting to be the person God had designed me to be, not the person I felt like I had to be in order to win people's approval. When I realized that God loved me, even in all of my insecurities, I discovered a freedom I'd never known, even after accepting Christ. When I started caring more about intimacy with God and less about the approval of man, I was able to begin speaking out more. I found that if I got a *truth* grounded deep in my spirit, it really didn't matter if people liked what I had to say or not. Truth was *truth*.

I also realized that confrontation isn't all bad. It's typically uncomfortable, but true *grace* involves confronting those things and mindsets that are not of God. It isn't love if a parent lets a toddler grab hold of a red hot pan. Likewise, it's not love to allow someone to remain in ignorance if I have an opportunity to speak about the *kingdom* into that person's situation.

Because I never wanted to come across as "bad" or "mean" to anyone, I simply never confronted anyone about anything—at least, not seriously. I argued fiercely in high school debates, but that doesn't count because there, I was *supposed* to confront. However, it was all based in performance orientation too. After carefully studying the life of Jesus, I realized that when he was truly passionate about something or when he wanted to guide those he loved, he didn't hold back his confrontation. He never confronted outside a spirit of *love* because he is *love* personified, but he had no problems whatsoever with confronting from inside that place of love.

The true test of my ability to speak out of this new spirit and attitude came when I was able to lovingly confront those with misperceptions. One memorable experience came while I was waiting in line at a local pharmacy to pick up a prescription for my dad. I have a special place in my heart for children. They're so un-jaded in most cases, and are honest without fail. I never take offense at a child's sincere questions because asking is the best way for them to receive a truthful answer to satisfy their curiosity. When I see a child looking, I make it a point to smile at them to remove their fears and to cut through the confusion of trying to reconcile what they're seeing. I look like the bionic woman to them, and the overall picture can be difficult for children to understand until they see the humanity in the midst of the machinery.

So I smile, and almost always, I will see their entire face light up with a return smile. I can also honestly say I've never had such an encounter turn out badly. The adults that accompany the kids can be a challenge though. Kids are honest. Adults are uncomfortable.

In this particular instance, a young girl about seven years old was in line with a woman who might have been her grandmother. I'm really not sure, but for the purpose of sharing this story, I'll make that supposition. They slipped into line beside me so quietly that at first I didn't even notice them. However, when I did, I saw that the little girl was looking at me. I smiled, and she instantly smiled back. She then turned to her grandmother and asked, "What happened to her?"

The question didn't remotely bother me. The grandmother's harsh and scolding answer profusely disturbed me though.

"Stop staring."

Embarrassingly, I have to admit that my first response was to want to fire off something about not being deaf, but I also didn't want to give a flesh-based knee-jerk reaction. I knew that she was just uncomfortable and, probably, embarrassed by the rather direct question. So I forced myself to stay calm. My frustration was based in knowing that such an answer only propagated a distanced view of anyone with a noticeable difference and would leave the child with an unsatisfied curiosity. Such things lead to assumptions and to a gross misunderstanding of circumstances. I didn't want this beautiful little girl to come to believe her questions were something to hide.

I turned and made direct eye contact with the grandmother.

"No, it's not a problem," I said.

Then with another smile, I directly addressed the beautifully innocent and naturally curious little girl.

"Hey, sweetheart."

As I expected, she broke into a smile. The grandmother's embarrassment was clearly apparent now, as she said, "She wanted to know what happened." That's something I've noticed. When confrontation is necessary, it forces others to address the things of which they've been fearful themselves.

I continued addressing the little girl directly, because it was *her* question I wanted to answer.

"When I was born, my muscles weren't strong enough for me to learn to walk as a baby. But I'm okay for now, sweetie. It's going to be just fine. Nothing is broken and nothing hurts."

Kids are content with the simple answers. They don't need the genetic breakdown or an explanation of generational curse breaking. Once their childlike curiosity and childlike faith are satisfied, then that's enough for them. The little girl smiled a gorgeous smile, nodded, and said, "Okay."

My intent was never to dishonor the grandmother, and I don't believe I did. My intent was to do what

Jesus did. When his disciples tried to keep children from coming to him, he instantly confronted his own followers and welcomed the children into his presence. He spoke of their position in the kingdom. Those who take the lowliest positions like that of a child are the greatest in the kingdom. My intent was to confront the mindset that would lead to misinformation about a situation. Who knows what the little girl would've been told after she left the store? But after I was willing and able to confront in love, I know that she heard the truth directly from me, and I know she did not leave the store being afraid to talk to someone who uses a wheelchair. I can only hope that her grandmother didn't scold her more after they left.

Through the grace or unmerited favor of God, we are made righteous through the *blood* of Christ. In Proverbs 28:1, we're told that "the righteous are as bold as a lion." It's not that we are righteous in and of ourselves. It's through Christ, and therefore, if we are living within the freedom of that identity, the boldness we have is not our own. It is the boldness of Jesus in us. That's why we can say what needs to be said without condemnation. As long as we say it from a place of love, even if it confronts, it will find its mark and bring to light the mindset that needs a change.

Recently, one of my friends laughed and said, "You weren't kidding when you said you've become more blunt and open! Girl, sometimes you flat out blow my hair back!"

She wasn't mad at me. Earlier, she had said she always wanted me to be up front with her in her walk.

So I am. And she is likewise with me. So when she made that statement, she was simply acknowledging how easy it is for me to say things now that in the past, I'd have held back.

Boldness is born of our acceptance of Christ in us. When we realize that we do nothing alone, and we do everything with his power at work through us, performance orientation and a desire to please others will cease and desist. A supernatural boldness will rise up and make us immune to the dividing voice of the enemy. And boldness doesn't always look like what we might expect. I am a little bit of fire on wheels. But there are different intensities of fire. And interestingly, the blue-white flame of directly ignited fuel burns significantly quieter than a raging red-orange wildfire. So most of the time, I'm not all that loud. But I'm no less passionate.

People often associate the concept of boldness with loudness and a jarring personality. But quite frankly, that's often not boldness at all. That's actually usually an attempt to convince oneself of the thing that person is screaming. Boldness at its foundation is a simple confidence in knowing that God is who he says he is; that he can be trusted, and that in the power of his infinite *grace*, we are everything he needs us to be to fulfill the plans he has for our lives. When we are confident that it is the plan of God and voice of the kingdom flowing from us, we develop a no-holds-barred approach to saying the things he wants to say through us. We can be faithful to his call because we've been delivered from our own definitions of what we think others expect of us.

Moments of Reflection

1. Are there areas in your life where you are "doing" more than "being"?

2. Is confrontation easy or difficult for you?

3. How do you avoid confronting out of flesh-based, knee-jerk reactions?

4. How do you personally deal with confrontation from inside a place of love?

5. What is true boldness and what does it look like for you?

Prayer of Refining

Dear Abba, thank you for the strength to be bold but also for the grace to confront only from inside a place of love. Make circumstances clear so that I have the wisdom to confront without letting my flesh or emotions take precedence. Show me how to seize the teachable moments and use them to bring glory to you. Lord, let me be so confident in you that I am unafraid to do the things that I know you have equipped me to do, even when it means taking an unpopular stand. Father, make me courageous, yet true to who you've designed me to be.

In the name of Jesus, so be it. Amen!

Jumping into the Flow

In 2000, I was working on my master's degree in public administration. All of the classes were in the evenings, a few evenings a week, so I was able to do the homework during daytime. Because of the way the schedule was arranged, some days there were no classes. On one of those afternoons, I sat at the computer typing an assignment for one of my classes. When I started to print it, I just sighed.

"I'm out of paper."

I closed my work and sat there, mildly frustrated, but not really too much so. I still had plenty of time to print it before class at the computer lab the next day. It was a mild nuisance, but certainly not the end of the world. I decided to find something else to do. My mom was busy with housework, Sissy was minding her own business, and Dad wasn't home from work yet.

You need computer paper.

The sudden impression was planted firmly in my spirit. But it had been an afternoon full of work and I was ready to take a break, so I tried to push off the impression. Even so, it kept growing in intensity. Finally, I realized it wasn't just my imagination. The Lord was speaking to my spirit.

"But God, I don't want to go get paper today."

The only office supply place in town was already closed, and there was no Wal-Mart in my hometown in those days, so buying paper would mean going to another town thirty minutes away. It was such a simple thing, but it seemed totally illogical to go that far for only a pack of paper. Still, I could not stop the feeling.

Finally, I wandered into the kitchen and asked Mom if she needed anything from the store, and like me, she did need a few items, but they could wait. By this time, Dad was home. I mentioned needing paper, and it was a beautiful early evening, so we decided to load up into the van and take an evening ride.

I asked the Lord what this was all about, and he suddenly became very specific.

"Go to Kmart. You'll park across from a blue car."

This was in the days before I was Spirit-baptized, and I'd never heard teachings on or explanations of words of knowledge, so this seemed like an unreal experience.

"But Lord, there might be a bunch of blue cars at Kmart, so how will I know which is the right one? Besides, I don't usually get my paper there."

His answer was strong, yet gentle.

"You'll know when you see it. And you're going to encourage the woman you meet."

I began to understand that this was about more than a pack of printer paper, and it had everything to do with carrying out a simple act of obedience, and not even totally for my benefit. It was now clear that this experience was for a greater purpose. So when my parents asked which store I wanted to go to, I told them Kmart. Feeling a little silly, I told them we were supposed to park across from a blue car. Of course, this piqued their curiosity, so I finally explained what I was experiencing, and to my surprise, they didn't doubt it at all.

The closer we got to Gainesville, the more my anticipation began to rise. At first, I had been highly skeptical, but all of those feelings began to fade. When we pulled into the parking lot, we began looking for a blue car, and as we neared the spot where we usually parked when we went to that particular store, I noticed that not only was the spot open, but also a blue car was in front of it. In fact, we all noticed at about the same time.

No one was in the car, and I was beginning to feel foolish again as we sat there and waited while I decided what to do. I was also starting to get nervous about the idea of approaching a woman I'd never met before to tell her God sent me to talk to her. By now, I was also trying to reason my way out of it. It might not even be a woman driving this particular blue car, right? Finally, I decided to scribble a quick note of generic encouragement, have my mom put it under the windshield wipers of the car, and then rush inside the store before anyone came out.

I got the note written and my mom and I got out of the van. I sighed in relief, and started to give the note to Mom.

"Lord, I tried." But he was silent.

I turned to look toward the building. At that exact moment, a woman stepped out of the store and started walking in our direction.

"Wait." His urging was so strong, yet not as much commanding as it was almost pleading, and I stopped

on the spot and knew this was the one he wanted to encounter. Mom saw what was happening and waited with me. Sure enough, the lady walked straight to the blue car. In that instant, I wanted to chicken out, and run. But I couldn't do it. So feeling a wee tad sheepish, I approached her.

I opened a simple conversation, then gave her the note after telling her I'd felt like God had led me to encourage the person in that car. She was astonished, and fought down tears as she told me that her son had been in a car accident some time before. He was now confined to a wheelchair, and he was having a hard time adjusting. She had some questions about accessible transportation and more things. Before the conversation was over, we had connected on a heart level, exchanged e-mail addresses and said our good-byes with a hug. Off and on for a while, we remained in touch via e-mail. We've lost touch now, but she and her son still cross my mind.

Long after that encounter was over, I found myself thinking about all that would have not happened if I hadn't obeyed. A lady in need of some information would've gone home without it. Oh sure, she might've found it another day and another time through another source. But it was a divinely appointed moment to share encouragement. The information was only secondary though. I would have missed the excitement and sheer blessing of having followed a string of clues to find a pearl of great price in God's heart. That encounter was as much, or maybe more, for me than it was for her after all in that respect. It was a firsthand glimpse into the adventure that even daily life could be with the leading of Holy Spirit.

Years later, I learned that what I had experienced were "words of knowledge," sometimes described as "clues," divinely downloaded by the Spirit of God himself to lead me to someone to whom he wanted to display his *love*. When I read Kevin Dedmon's book, *The Ultimate Treasure Hunt*, in the fall of 2008, I was stoked to discover that there are groups who do entire outreaches by doing nothing but follow clues.

All of these experiences have been tender things the Lord has used to teach me that there are times when my analytical mind is useful, but there are times when it can be a hindrance. He's been gently and lovingly teaching me how to flow in his Spirit. The Word teaches us that Jesus was *love* incarnate, so we can safely infer that everything Jesus did was from that place of *love*. There were times when he did "blow people's hair back," but there were times when his actions were as gentle as the *lamb* he is. Some people call it tempering. Some call it balance. I've come to see it as flow. There are times when being gentle is appropriate, but there are also times when blowing your hair back is appropriate. The wisdom to know how to respond comes purely from being spirit-led at all times. Learning to flow is an indicator of our ability to hear as well as our obedience to do the appropriate thing in the moment.

When we're placed on this earth, God has very specific purposes for us. We often think we have to figure it all out. We tend to think that somehow our finite analytical reasoning can make sense of and figure out an infinite God's divine plans. But the truth is that it's a bit like trying to empty the Mississippi River one cup full at a time, and as long as we continue to function in that mentality, we will only hinder the progress of what he wants to do in and through us. We can either follow him as he leads, trusting him to be the guide who sees through the darkness, or we can go around the same mountain again and again until we realize that God himself wants to guide us on a specific path. He doesn't want to send us some kind of trained tour guide to lead us like a surrogate. The same one who planned every detail of our lives now wants to personally walk with us step by step through those plans. It's incredible really. The key to being able to embrace this radically spirit-led lifestyle is in simply surrendering to his leading.

This has been one of the single most difficult parts of my walk with him. Because I worked so hard in academics, I developed that analytical mindset very early on. However, my inability to flow was actually much deeper than that.

It is all about trust. Because of feeling so worthless for so long, I had developed a basic distrust of everyone and an unhealthy skepticism of almost everything. When those two partnering issues cloud your view, you simply cannot see that it's not even about trusting people. It's about trusting God. And it's about trusting ourselves.

In 2 Corinthians 4:4 (NASB), we're told that "the god of this world has blinded the minds of the unbelieving so that they might not see the light of the gospel of the glory of Christ, who is the image of God." I distinctly remember the moment that particular passage gelled for me. I was sitting in my pastor's office, discussing a particular issue with him.

"Holly, people are blinded. It's not that they *won't* see. It's that they *can't*. They're spiritually blinded. All we can do is pray that the *truth* is illuminated so they can get into a place of being able to see."

I sat there, almost stunned, as that piece of *truth* was illuminated to me.

Over a period of a couple of years, I increasingly realized that when we fail to trust him, what we actually are doing is "unbelieving" that he is able to keep us protected. So even if we believe in him and have accepted him as Savior, in those areas we're holding back from trusting him, we're still living in unbelief. As such, we've opened the door to spiritual blindness that will obscure our view of the glory of Christ in those areas of life.

I began asking him to illuminate all areas in which I needed to see the glory of Christ where I hadn't seen it before. In retrospect, I realized what I was really asking him to do was to reveal all areas of unbelief in my life. To this day, he's still revealing areas, and I figure he'll continue those revelations until I draw my last breath.

Indiana Jones movies are some of my absolute favorites. In *Indiana Jones and the Last Crusade*, one of the greatest illustrations of the concept of learning to trust and flow comes near the end. Indiana stands at the edge of a precipice, looking over a chasm that looks impossible to cross. All he has is his scribbled archaeological journal, and an image of a man stepping out into thin air, trusting that his feet will land surely on something when it looks like nothing is there. On the other side of the chasm is healing.

I've found in my own life that this very principle is true. When we look at the picture of what the Lord is asking us to do, even if it looks impossible, but we do it in obedience anyway, we do find healing on the other side of the chasm of unbelief. Trust always ultimately leads to healing, and to the ability to flow freely in the power of the Holy Spirit.

Moments of Reflection

1. What is your initial reaction when God asks you to do something unusual?

2. When you were obedient even when it seemed unusual, what was the effect on your confidence?

3. What things has He asked you to do that you just have not been able to do yet?

4. When you think of these things, what is it that is holding you back from moving forward with them?

5. How do you believe God is asking you to flow forward next?

Prayer of Refining

Dear Abba, thank you for being my sure thing when I feel you asking me to step out in faith. Remind me that if you are asking me to do something, you are already present in the circumstance. You aren't going to ask me to do something and then desert me. You are so faithful. Father, illuminate the areas in which I am still holding onto unbelief, and reveal to me the ways you have empowered me with all it takes to flow in your Holy Spirit.

In the name of Jesus, so be it. Amen!

Sharing the Journey

The Lord can and does use radical experiences in our lives to lead to our healing from trauma. However, it is most often the combination of the mundane *and* the radical that leads to the most comprehensive healing in our lives. This is one of the most valuable lessons I have learned over time. There are the "suddenlies," but there is also the slow-but-steady process that culminates in the fulfillment of our destinies. It's in the process that we often tend to feel pressure to give up, but what we tend to fail to notice is that it is also in the process where we really "grow up" in our faith. It is also the process we tend to want to avoid the most. It can be painful, and no one likes to voluntarily sign up for pain. What I've discovered though is that the process really isn't designed to be painful. It is designed by a loving Father whose heart is not to inflict pain, but rather to free us from those things that hinder. It is our kicking and screaming that makes the process painful.

Corrie ten Boom once said, "Hold everything in your hands lightly, otherwise it hurts when God pries our hands open." I'm not implying that God delights in ripping things from our grasp, but I totally agree with this mighty kingdom woman. A lot of people misuse scripture, but one of the most unfortunate out-of-context misuses I see on a regular basis is a part of Job 1:21 (KJV):

The Lord giveth and the Lord taketh away.

People make it sound as if the Lord, in his sovereignty, gives and takes at his will. There is assuredly truth in that…he does. But he never does it out of a "just because I am God" motivation. Instead, everything he does is from a place of unconditional love. Everything he does is based on the absolute best he has planned for us. When he "removes something from our hands," it isn't because he wants to leave our hands empty. It's because he wants to place something even more precious there. In Romans 8:28 (NASB), we are reminded that we can "know that God causes all things to work together for good to those who love God, to those who are called according to *His* purpose." This means that no matter what we face in life, he is not taken aback. He is never surprised, and can redeem any situation.

People often ask me how I keep the attitude in life that I do despite what appear to be radically unfair circumstances. My first answer is that no one sees me one hundred percent of the time except God. Even my friends and family don't know all the times I fall apart. But he does, and he knows my attitude is not always Georgia peachy perfect. My second answer is that I have to keep perspective. No, my life ain't a bowl of cherries. But show me someone whose life is? We all have our own flavors of challenge, and we get to make daily decisions on what we are going to do with them.

Something I learned a long time ago is that how we react to circumstances greatly influences the overall outcome. And it is those reactions that are true indicators of how much we trust God in any given situation. Jesus had to trust his Father a *lot*. He, the perfectly sinless Son, willfully gave up his place in Heaven for a season on Earth in order to bring redemption to the entire human race. If he had not been able to trust Abba, he could not have taken one step into the boundaries of time. Imagine for a minute the child who steps onto a school bus for the first day of kindergarten. That child is going to a different place, a new experience, and a new season of life. And that child also has a simple trust that when school is over, the bus will bring him home, and once there, he will be greeted by the parents from whom he was separated for a time. That's sort of how it must have been for that season for Jesus. He stepped out of heaven, trusting that he would return and that his immortality downgraded to mortality would be restored.

He didn't say, "Oh, Abba, please don't make me go. Please send someone else."

He said, "Here I am. Send me."

Jesus was even willing to hold heaven lightly so that when his destiny stood before him, he could release it without his father having to pry his fingers open. Now that, my friends, is trust—releasing a grip on heaven to be sent to earth to restore access to heaven for others. Wow.

That's how it has to be for us. When we have a circumstance at hand, God will use that very thing to bring freedom to others if we let him. He will frequently use those things to shape our outlook to make us ready to reach out. Jesus was fully God, but he had to become fully man in order to experience firsthand the condition of mankind. People on earth knew God only through the lenses of the law, and did not have a concept of him on a personal level. He was present, yet distant. In his sovereign plan, he must have seen it as important to bring redemption through relationship based on a common experience. It wasn't enough to him to bring a quick, tidy fix, though I feel sure he probably could have. Yet if he had, it's not so much that he wouldn't have understood the human condition as it is that humans wouldn't have understood the *grace* of a loving God.

That's the example I've tried to live by. Do I believe that God created me with physical challenges on purpose? No. In fact, I'd go so far as to say that to believe that is a deception from the pit. It would make *no* sense for an earthly father to say, "Come here, honey, let me break your legs, arms, and spine, to help you become a better person and an inspirational example for others." And if even an imperfect father on earth would never do that, why in heaven would a loving Abba do such a thing? Yet, do I believe that he has provided redemption for it by making even those challenges work together for good? Absolutely. There are things we go through in life that might seem unfair or frustrating. However, if we never experience those things, we would never be able to empathize with those hurting around us.

For me, as a Spirit-filled believer, the hard part for a long time was trying to reconcile what appeared to be two polar opposites. On one hand, I believe in total healing made possible by the victory of Christ. I have experienced having some of the most anointed people on this planet pray for me and my miracle, and I know with every fiber of my being that those prayers moved the heart of God. Some of the most impacting prayers to me have been the prayers that children have prayed over me. Their pure and childlike faith stirs my faith on a level that few other prayers can. Yet on the other hand, I see myself and others like me who choose to still believe while having not yet experienced the manifestation of a miracle. Some people ask me if that shakes my faith, and my honest answer is no, it doesn't. It can't. The word is clear that, "faith is confidence in what we hope for and assurance about what we do not see" (Hebrews 11:1, NIV). Do I always understand it all? Of course, not. I am human, and a foolish one at that. So I stopped trying to understand, and remind myself, sometimes not daily, but instead hourly, that it is best to rest in God's promises. I can't make them happen before their due time. Abraham already tried that and look what happened.

Children praying for me at the International Institute
of Mentoring in Cleveland, Tennessee.

For a long time, the enemy tried to use the fact that I haven't yet experienced the manifestation of a creative miracle against me to disqualify me from praying for healing for others. I felt like a hypocrite or like somehow my own faith would be discredited. Worse yet, in my foolishness, I worried that my not yet having received a miracle might make God look bad, as if it appeared he lied. Silly me to think that I have any bearing on God's reputation. Looking back, I have to laugh at myself. Then one day I watched an interview with Heidi Baker, who cofounded Iris Ministries with her husband. She said that sometimes, they pray for the blind and their eyes are opened. But sometimes they aren't, and that's why they also open homes for the blind. Furthermore, they also involve those who aren't yet able to see in ministry and prayers for others, and those blind individuals take great joy in knowing that God is using them to minister to and encourage others. In fact, sometimes when those individuals pray for others, the others become recipients of instant miracles.

For years, I've looked up to Heidi and the radical way she has immersed herself in the heart of God by ministering to "the least of these." So when I realized she didn't have a problem with the fact that not all receive instant miracles and that they are still valuable to God in ministering to others, I was so liberated. In fact, the night I watched that interview, I felt so relieved that I cried, and I knew that I could move forward in my own callings. For the first time, I didn't care anymore when people questioned me, nor did I feel useless any longer.

There was no more self-condemnation, wondering, "Holly, who do you think you are?"

Up until then, I had steered my focus on international outreach away from providing medical gear to the disabled. Under my old mindset, it wasn't acceptable to provide wheelchairs or prosthetics for people if what I really wanted was to see people receive healing. It had seemed double-minded to consider it, or as mentioned earlier, it even felt hypocritical. But after seeing the interview that changed my mind, I realized that the truly hypocritical thing to do would be to go on having my own wheelchair to empower me in the waiting while not reaching out to others who could benefit from the same technology. So I opened my heart to it, and while I've not yet begun such a medical outreach, I have begun the process of narrowing the focus to specific areas of need. What I have discovered is that the needs are *vast*, and I believe this is an area in which the Lord plans to use me in the future. God's purposes and plans will be revealed in time. Some will receive miracles instantly, but for those who don't, I want to do what I can to make their lives more comfortable and fruitful while they wait—while we wait together. That's the essence of true evangelism. I want to meet them where they are because that's what Jesus did. He met people at their point of need.

Moments of Reflection

1. What has God removed from your hands and what has he replaced it with?

2. How did it make you feel to have those things removed?

3. Have you released any negativity that you might have experienced toward God in the removal season? If so, how?

4. How did it make you feel to have the "better than" placed in your hands?

5. Have you thanked God for that exchange? If so, how?

Prayer of Refining

Dear Abba, I praise you for being the abundant life-giver. From this point forward, I choose to recognize that you only give me abundant life in exchange for the things I've held onto. I know that whatever you want to give me is far greater than anything you might ask me to let go of. I also recognize and acknowledge that it is in these divine exchanges that I find the places where I can have true compassion and empathy with others. I am able to use my own experiences to help level the path for others as they walk through their own mountains and valleys. Lord, thank you for your abundant life.

In the name of Jesus, so be it. Amen!

Discovering Joy Unspeakable and Full of Glory

Meeting people at their point of need does require a commitment to growth on the part of those who are reaching out. However, the sticking point is not so much that we are committed to growth based on our own intentional focus as it is based on our trust of his love and inherent goodness. Receiving goes beyond believing. When we truly *receive* the revelation of his love and goodness, we cannot help but find ourselves squarely in the middle of a paradigm shift. Prior to that revelation, we operate out of a place of works. We operate out of more of a sense of obligation than out of the overflow of his abundant grace in our own lives. But when that shift comes, we realize that he is fully alive even in our weaknesses and failures, and that even though we are weak and have no doubt failed, he chose us and loved us *anyway*! When we are firmly convinced of that unshakeable affection and true joy, the river of living water begins to flow out from us.

> Now on the last day, the great day of the feast, Jesus stood and cried out, saying, "If anyone is thirsty, let him come to Me and drink. He who believes in Me," as the Scripture said, "From his innermost being will flow rivers of living water."
>
> John 7:37–38 (NASB)

That is one of the passages that I've returned to many times throughout the years. We have an open invitation to come to him and drink. We do not drink of his spirit one time and then are done with it. We can return to him over and over, knowing that this river still flows. There is no drought or drying up. And because we have an abundant supply available to us, we can rest in the assurance that we can also continue to pour it out to others. That is, as long as we remember to come to him and drink again when we need it.

I drink from the river often.

I have to drink from the *river often*. I do what I can to keep a happy face, but I definitely have my limits. So my joy *has* to come from a source more plentiful than my own emotions can provide. Fortunately, God well knows that and is still full of grace.

If I am going to share my testimony, I have to be raw and honest. The challenges of my life have cost me a lot. For example, I have had to lay on the altar of my heart the sacrifice of not having biological children. In eighth grade, in one class, we were required to make a list of five, ten, and fifteen year goals. I remember having a five-year goal of having graduated from high school and being in college. My ten year goals included having graduated college, obtained a good job, and gotten married. And on the fifteen- year list was to have children, whether biological or adopted. That meant by my late twenties, I had wanted to be a mother to at least two children.

As time moved forward, I had focused on academics and due to all those insecurity issues mentioned in previous chapters, not so much on personal relationships aside from friends. So high school years came and went, as did college. I got the job I never even imagined I'd have. Yet in all that, there was no focus on marriage or children. Really, there was only one romantic relationship that I'd have said counted. Sure there were crushes and teenage heartthrobs, and there was one particular friendship, which I guess I'd call a "might have been." Over the years, I've tried not to wonder too much how that one could have gone. So if I had to drum it down to basics, only one went so far as being labeled a "relationship" as people like to label things, so in that light, it's the only one that I'd have said mattered. After a short period of seeing where it went, it fell apart. What had begun as a fantastic years-long friendship in college that morphed into a relationship out of college with what seemed to be potential dissolved into nothing. It was a difficult season in which not only had I found myself back outside a relationship, but also I had lost the best friend who'd been my closest confidant for probably four years. Where we once talked for hours on end and spent as much time together as possible, we faded into nothing and never even talked. Then he moved out of state, further cementing the fact that it just wasn't meant to continue. That seemed to validate my opinion that I was pretty much worthless in those days when it came to the marriage issue. It was right after that happened when I got a job teaching college. So I threw my everything into that job. It was a really good distraction from romance, and I was really good at being really distracted from it!

So I was extremely busy with work, my students, my family, my friends and the activities I liked being involved with. In my mid-twenties, it began to hit me hard that I had reached that "fifteen years from middle school" season, and according to my desired schedule, I was five years behind on getting married and having a young family. The fifteen year goal mark came and went, and to be really raw and honest, I went through a season of severe depression about this. Even more raw and honest is that some of the people closest to me probably never even knew. Some may find out about that deep dark struggle for the first time as they read this.

During that season, I looked at baby furniture, clothes, and gear, daydreaming of what it might be like to decorate a nursery. I had several friends and acquaintances with disabilities, who were married and already had small children, or they were having their first ones. They were all sharing stories of how their friends and family were surrounding them to help with the parts of child care they couldn't physically do, and all the while leaving the "mommy" role to them. It had been so refreshing to see the collaboration. It gave me hope, yet it was bittersweet. After all, I wasn't even near a marriage, much less parenthood, but it was nice to think ahead and dream.

Also around that time, my niece was pregnant with her first child, and two years later, with her second, so in some ways, I got to expend some of my baby fever on buying things for my great-nephew and great-niece.

When Conner was born, I remember holding him for the first time, probably not more than fifteen minutes after he was born. He was so perfect, and I was awestruck at the beauty of new life. I couldn't help but marvel at God's majestic creativity. And I was so joyful to hold this sweet baby and just look at him. But no one knew that mixed with tears of joy celebrating his birth were tears of longing to hold a child of my own. One of the things I had always wanted to do was to pray over my child, prophetically declaring God's promises over that child's life.

So when Conner was about two or three months old, I remember sitting in my living room, holding him tightly swaddled against me as my mother did my niece's hair. I looked at every detail of his beautiful face, and unsure of what my own future held regarding holding a child of my own, I quietly declared the promises of God over his life, knowing that there are plenty of promises for all, including any future children God might bring into my life. In those moments of declaring promises over Conner, I felt some of the heaviness of not knowing lift from me. It was in releasing a blessing that I finally experienced relief for my own soul.

When Chloe was born a couple of years later, I prayed for her too. At that point, some of those feelings resurfaced, but by that time, I had surrendered most of them to God for healing. I still felt somewhat inferior to those my age and even far younger who had families, but I had begun to find peace, knowing that God's plans would never be disappointing. Even if they looked different than I had planned, they would be beautiful. So that was my new focus.

One particularly healing event happened for me during church on Mother's Day in my early thirties. Our pastor called forward to bless them all the mothers and those who wanted to be mothers someday, and for the obvious reason, of course, I did not go forward. Then, totally surprising me, one sweet little lady and a friend of mine from the congregation came over to me.

She said, "I think you need to go up there."

I really didn't want to at first because I didn't see any point in it, and I felt a little embarrassed due to my own remaining insecurities with the concept. But she said, "I don't know what God has for your future, honey, but whether you have children or not, you are already a mother figure to many."

I had certainly never thought of it like that. Then I remembered an earlier prophetic word I had received about being a mother to the nations, and I realized that I had too narrowly defined my own role. So I felt a new joy I'd never felt.

Conner, my "Boogie," loves to ride on my back.

*Chloe, my "Shoogie," learned from her big
brother at an early age how to ride.*

Then much to my own surprise one day, I discovered that my outlook had entirely changed. In fact, I had experienced almost a one-hundred-eighty degree turnaround in my maternal desires. Suddenly, I *loved* being an aunt who could be goofy and crazy with two kids and feel no pain of regret for myself. I saw the beauty of raising children, but I no longer had any real desire whatsoever to become an actual parent, or not to be either. If it happened, it happened, and if it didn't, it didn't. Either way, I was at peace. I had reached that point of surrender. Sometimes, as mentioned earlier, we let go of things kicking and screaming, but when we release them into God's hands, we see things from a totally different perspective.

I began to receive words about joy from people gifted in the prophetic. Interestingly, they weren't words about "getting" joy, but instead, they were words about already "having" joy. At one conference I attended, the lady minister looked deep into my eyes and said she could see that I had chosen not to be bitter, that by natural circumstances, I had every reason to be bitter, and yet I had chosen not to be. It was a sweet moment, hearing from a prophetic teacher who was hearing from Abba. And he was telling her that he saw my heart wasn't bitter. It made me all the more grateful for his grace.

I attended another meeting, this time, a fivefold ministry gathering in Rock Hill, South Carolina, in February 2012. I knew quite a number of the people there, but there were also quite a few I did not know. The evening was full of the flow of the Holy Spirit and people were receiving blessings left and right. One of my friends was leading worship, and after a period of time, he flowed into playing "Holy Ground," which happens to be one of my longtime favorites. He sang part of it, and then was joined by a woman who is the spiritual mother to a mutual friend of ours. As she started singing while he played, I couldn't help but smile. I had never met her before that night, but I could tell that her love for Jesus was deep. More often than not, during worship, I have my eyes closed. I love finding myself only in his presence, virtually unaware of what people around me are doing. But I was so drawn by her depth of worship that my eyes were open, and I was smiling and watching her. She began singing the second verse, specifically the words, "In his presence, I know there is joy beyond all measure." Our eyes met, and still flowing with the music, she said, "You know that joy, don't you?" Still smiling, possibly even smiling more, I nodded and mouthed the words, "Yes, I do."

It's true. I *do* know that joy. Some would say it is because I know Jesus, and I agree. But I'd be quick to point out that the deeper reason I know joy is because Jesus knows me. And he loves me—*a lot*. So I have a lot of love to share freely. I drink from the River of Life often, and I want to share that life and love with everyone I possibly can. Nothing, no human desire or dream of my own, will ever trump that desire to pour into others what he has so abundantly poured into me. Whomever and whatever else he brings into my life is just icing on the cake. What I want most now is to see my freedom to drink from the *river* compel others to run and drink too and know him personally.

Moments of Reflection

1. When was a time when you realized you were lacking joy in a particular circumstance?

2. How has God restored it to you?

3. What is your favorite "song of joy"?

4. How do you personally "drink from the river"?

5. What are some ways you might be able to minister joy unspeakable and full of glory to someone in need of it?

Prayer of Refining

Dear Abba, thank you for being my complete joy unspeakable and full of glory. You are the sovereign redeemer gives me joy in often unexpected ways. I am grateful that you give us songs of joy for every circumstance that has appeared unredeemable. Remind me, Lord, to drink deeply and to drink often from the river of your presence. Make me aware of others and be able to respond to their heart cries. Make me a minister of your joy!

In the name of Jesus, so be it. Amen!

Embracing a Royal Position

When the joy of the Lord becomes our strength, it puts other things in perspective. The more we walk in the revelation that our lives are *all* in his strength rather than our own, the freer we become. We can truly do no good thing outside his empowerment to do so. That process of revelation is exceedingly liberating. Everything of value in our lives is born of direct relationship with him, and the closer we dare to go in relationship with him, the deeper in the center of his destiny for our lives we will find ourselves. When we let go of our old thinking patterns in order to become spirit-led, we have in effect, allowed him to take us to a new level.

God, as a loving Father, has made it clear by his word that with regard to relationship, he has made the way for us to become sons of God.

> For all who are being led by the Spirit of God, these are sons of God. For you have not received a spirit of slavery leading to fear again, but you have received a spirit of adoption as sons by which we cry out, "Abba! Father!" The Spirit Himself testifies with our spirit that we are children of God, and if children, heirs also, heirs of God and fellow heirs with Christ, if indeed we suffer with Him so that we may also be glorified with Him.
>
> Romans 8:14–17 (NASB)

Don't worry, ladies…daughters are "sons" too! Us chickees are not excluded!

> There is neither Jew nor Greek, there is neither slave nor free man, there is neither male nor female; for you are all one in Christ Jesus.
>
> Galatians 3: 28 (NASB)

God began to reveal to me the empowering and humbling reality of sonship a few years ago. Sonship is one of the most incredible gifts we could have been given. It wasn't enough for God just to save us. He wanted to adopt us into his own family. That meant he also wanted us to be his family, complete with all of the "perks" of being the son (daughter) of a king. Everything possible that's available to a person born in the king's household is available to us who are adopted (or born *again*) into the king's household.

This part of the journey for me began with a season in which God kept giving me dreams about jewelry in the night. Anyone who knows me well knows that I enjoy me some bling. I don't overdo it, but I really enjoy jewelry. So during the season when he began teaching me about sonship, he spoke to me using jewelry. In several of the dreams, I was in various stores looking at unique pieces. In another, someone placed a piece on my wrist. In yet another, I was following a set of instructions to assemble some gemstones, and it became a stunning ring. Upon waking from each dream, I realized God, as a father, was showing me how he viewed me as royalty, specifically as "Daddy's princess."

With each new revelation, I fell further into the identity he had created for me. So many of the old obstacles in how I viewed myself dropped off of me, like unshackled chains falling off to set a prisoner free. I got it down deep in my spirit that I am a daughter of the Most High King, not because of anything I have done or have not done, but rather because of the reality of an identity rebuilt in Jesus. I am now passionate about sharing with people that when we learn and actually receive our position as sons in the kingdom, we realize that the identity we've had for ourselves for a lifetime is not usually the identity that is *truly* ours through Christ. This immensely changes the way we move forward. Things can never be the same. God is far more interested in who we are than in what we do. Sonship comes with an understanding that he loves spending time with us "just because" it is a position of knowing him, not just on an occasional basis, but in all things at all times.

One of the New Testament parables that I enjoy in particular is the parable of the prodigal son. I believe that for most of us, we can relate to wearing the prodigal's sandals. In the parable, both sons were the Father's and always had been. The son who never left home had a real issue with the brother who squandered his inheritance. I'm of the mindset that this parable was a picture of those who were considered "top of the bunch" in the church of those times. The religious Jews had a difficult time accepting that Gentiles, who were considered heathens and much like the prodigal son, had a place of esteem in the king's palace. The Jews saw themselves as "the sons who'd never strayed." And true, they were to a degree…but the prodigals, the Gentiles, were just as welcomed. All along, the Lord had loved all of mankind. Otherwise, he'd never have sent a Savior, once for *all*. But aside from this view of the prodigal son's parable, there is the more traditional view of it as a story of redemption. We can seek for fulfillment outside our father's house. Yet in the end, we will forever have all of what we need inside his house. When we realize that we need only to go directly to him for everything, we will find the freedom of knowing him as "father."

In addition to that story, there is a modern day parable that is especially poignant for me. It's my favorite Disney story, *The Little Mermaid*. All Ariel wanted was to experience another life, specifically life on land with working legs instead of life as a mermaid under the surface of the ocean. She went to great lengths to collect items from a life she desired, daydreaming of all that might be. Determined to experience that life, she took things into her own hands, going to "the dark side" to make a trade. She gave up her voice in exchange for a time-limited chance to live her dream. Part of the deal was that she got what she wanted, but for only three days, during which time she had to win the prince's heart and receive "the kiss of true love." If she succeeded, she'd get her heart's desire in permanent form. If she failed, she'd return to the ocean and belong to Ursula. Most of us have seen the movie and know the story. I remember the first time I saw it…how I was struck with the deeper meaning. In later years, I marveled at how prophetically parabolic it was.

For me, of course, there is the interesting comparison to wanting "legs that work." In that regard, I can relate to the feeling, and silly though it might sound, that movie encouraged me to remember that it's okay to ask God directly for a miracle. Even moreso though, there is the prophetic picture of "losing our voice" when we choose to seek to fulfill our hearts' desires in our own ways. That's what happens when we compromise —We lose our voice. Ironically, it was Ariel's voice that had caused Prince Eric to fall in love with her in the first place. When she saved his life and was singing over him, while she was still a mermaid, he knew nothing else about her, but he heard that voice. Then it was that very thing she had to sacrifice to try to win his heart as a human. And even more ironically, when Ariel just *almost* managed to get that kiss, it was her own voice used against her as Ursula, the enemy, intervened to cause a definitive failure. What we don't often realize is that sacrificing our voice (our gifts) leads to a struggle based in works, and just as Ariel failed, we do too. We can't make things happen. So we need a rescuer, and even after we're captured in bondage as a result of our own failures, Jesus is faithful as that rescuer. In the movie, it is the father king who rescues his wayward daughter.

Sitting out on the water, resting in his grace.

My favorite part of the movie (well, aside from all the fantastic music!) is a scene at the very end, after Ariel has become a mermaid again. She's sitting on a rock in the ocean, watching Prince Eric on shore. Unbeknownst to her, her father, the king, is watching. There is no pretense. Just a girl, watching the guy she loves, wishing she had a future with him. And her father saw the genuine desires of her heart. He then places his scepter on the surface of the water; power emanating from it reaches her, transforms her fins into legs, and enables her to live her dream…this time also keeping the gift of her voice—truth without compromise. Her father and king had had the power to transform her all along. All she'd have had to do was ask him.

Isn't that true of all of us? When we cease from striving before our Father, the King, he already sees the desires of our hearts. Actually, he sees them whether we cease or not, and if our delight is in him, those desires are *from* him. Furthermore, if we trust our path in life to him, trusting him, he will bring those desires to fruition.

> Delight yourself also in the Lord, and He will give you the desires and secret petitions of your heart. Commit your way to the Lord [roll and repose each care of your load on Him]; trust (lean on, rely on, and be confident) also in Him and He will bring it to pass.
>
> Psalm 37:4–5 (AMP)

Our sonship is not revoked by prodigality. It might be delayed, but if we are willing to return to him, even when we've really messed up, we are welcomed home with open arms. He will pull out all the stops, hold a celebration, clothe us in clean garments (representing righteousness) and putting new sandals on our feet (symbolizing covenant and peace). He isn't afraid of the cleanup job if we aren't afraid of repentance. Even the prodigal one was willing to settle for a life of service, "earning his keep" so to speak, but the father wanted him as his *son*. It didn't matter what he had done or not done. All that mattered was that he was safe and back in his father's arms. That's what he wants for all of us.

Sonship has to do with really coming to understand what it means to live in the grace of Jesus. It has to do with acknowledging that while God is a Holy and Sovereign King, He is also a tender, loving and yes, even funny Father. When we live our relationship with him only as King, we see him only as the Lord of the Law. In this mindset, we are usually more concerned with earning God's favor and trying to stay in his favor. Such a relationship can be based in fear, which is not from God. We're actually told that "perfect love casts out fear" (1 John 4:18 NASB). However, with a Father King, through *grace* revelation, we begin to live with a totally different motivation. We are motivated by love for him rather than by a need to be loved by him. One's needs cease when they are fulfilled. So when we realize that *he loves us*, we no longer lack his love. So our focus shifts to fulfilling what Jesus called the two greatest commandments: loving God and loving others. That's how we know if we really are sons of God.

> This is how we know who the children of God are and who the children of the devil are: Anyone who does not do what is right is not God's child, nor is anyone who does not love their brother and sister.
>
> 1 John 3:10 (NIV)

Sonship is an incredible reality. In fact, I am confident that the victory we experience in our lives will be dependent upon how we view the Father. There is so much difference in going to him as a Father rather than going to him as a judge only. And when we can go to him as Abba, there is nothing we can't discuss with him. I say discuss because prayer is a conversation. We talk sometimes, but we also listen while he talks. I mentioned earlier that my family says I was born talking and never stopped. Well, imagine my delight when I realized that I can converse in prayer with God anytime, all the time, whenever and wherever I want!

He loves hearing me and talking with me, and I love it too. However, in prayer, I've discovered that I probably should listen more than I talk! But when we do talk, there's no topic that is off limits. There is nothing too trivial, too silly, or too big for his attention. To some, this will sound heretical, but I've even gone to him about a baby passing gas! A friend's sweet grandbaby had experienced a major intestinal problem for which surgery was required, and afterwards, the doctors had said if the baby could start passing gas, it meant healing was happening. So to Abba I went.

"Lord, thank You for her healing. Help that baby poot!"

And guess what? She did! I'm not claiming it was just because of my prayers. A lot of us were praying that. So God heard those authentic prayers, though some people would find that a terrible thing to ask before a holy King. And to those people, I'd say, "But I was asking that of my Father." He is that close and loving that he is attentive to every detail of life, even a tiny newborn with tummy troubles.

One of the most interesting things he's revealed to me about sonship and my royal inheritance is that the greater revelation I have of who he is, the more I discover who I am *and* the less I have to know all at the same time. Most of us spend huge portions of our lives searching, trying to discover who we are or what our purpose in life is. But when we begin to focus more on just knowing who he is, our own identities come into focus right at the same time we are content enough in him—that it's no longer a driving need to know. All that matters is him and his purposes.

Moments of Reflection

1. What are the benefits of sonship in your life?

2. What are the personal ways God reminds you of your royal position?

3. What is something in your life that you have tried to obtain by your own efforts?

4. What happened when you released it to God?

5. How does knowing that you are a son change how you are able to approach the Lord with your prayers?

Prayer of Refining

Dear Abba, thank you that I can freely come to you as just that—my Abba Father! Knowing you as my king is amazing, but having the freedom to know you as my father is overwhelming. I am so grateful. Show me how to walk in the authority that comes with my royal position. Reveal to me areas where I've seen myself only as a slave and renew my mind, Lord, so that I may embrace the fullness of who I am in you.

In the name of Jesus, so be it. Amen!

Unlocking the
Power of Forgiveness

The Bible is clear that forgiveness is an integral piece of the overall picture of redemption in people's lives. It's a two-way street. We are both forgiven and expected to forgive. Most believers have experienced teaching on this concept. However, its translation to practicality is where we have a hard time. It's one thing to read a textbook, but it's another thing entirely to take the lab practical and pass. Then beyond that, it's even entirely a different thing to be out of school, in the "real world," and being able to use that concept in a live situation.

It's like reading about how to start an IV line, then practicing on a laboratory mannequin, then practicing on classmates, and then being a licensed nurse starting an IV on a patient in a hospital. It's a progression of growth. It's no different really when it comes down to applying biblical principles, including forgiveness. I found this out firsthand in May 2010.

I was going to get my nails done, and since the salon I like to use is inside a particular Walmart, my mother was going to get a few groceries while I was in the salon. My dad and my sister were going to sit in Bertha, my van, and wait for us. Every woman knows the difficulty of digging into a wallet with "freshly did" nails. Remember I'm an analytical thinker though, right? So I tried to plan ahead by asking my dad to pull a $20 bill from my wallet so I could lay it on my tray and therefore avoid the problem. He did, and I wheeled inside. Sometimes when I go into the salon, if it is too crowded and the wait is going to be too long, I'll just wait and go back another day. This was the case on that day. There was going to be a long wait, so I decided just to go with Mom to get groceries. I also wanted to pick up some lip gloss anyway, so I didn't mind delaying the nail procedure.

As my mother looked at some produce, I felt a slight tug at the back of my chair. Actually, it was so slight that if I wasn't so used to what feels "normal" with the chair, I'd never have noticed. But I did, so I whirled around, but saw no one near. My purse was supposed to be on the back of my chair, so I asked Mom to check to see that it was still there. When she said it was, I asked her to see if my wallet was inside it.

"No! It isn't!" she said.

I backtracked through the immediate area where we were to see if it had fallen out, but it was nowhere to be seen. I'm pretty even keeled, so I didn't panic. Instead, I just tried to think of what to do next. I had no proof that someone had just snatched it. I also remembered that I had asked Dad to hand me that $20 bill out of it while still in the van. So I handed Mom the few items I had on my tray and told her I'd be right back, that I wanted to go see if Dad had just laid my wallet on the seat beside him instead of putting it back in my purse.

When I got to the van, he searched, and he said he had placed it back in my purse. So sure enough, it was not in the vehicle anywhere. So I went back into the store and met back up with my mother, and got my lip gloss tubes back. Still not wanting to believe I'd just been robbed, I told her it was still possible it had just fallen out of the purse. We agreed to split up and retrace our steps to search for it, looking from the front of the store to the back, meeting up on the back aisle.

I started in the direction I had chosen, and before I had even gotten to the end of the first aisle, I heard a woman cry out.

"That girl took my wallet!"

At first, no one seemed to pay attention, but knowing that my own wallet was missing, I turned quickly to look in the direction she was indicating. She yelled out again, this time more urgently, and was moving as fast as she could, but it was obvious her knee was in pain.

"Somebody stop her! Somebody, help! I can't run fast enough to catch her…she took my wallet!"

When I saw her pointing to a girl, something registered in my mind. I remembered seeing the young girl a few minutes before I felt that tug at the back of my chair. When the girl realized she had been identified, she took off running. I zipped into high speed, flying after her, knowing that I had to try to think of a way to cut her off, because there was no way I could overtake her. The pursuit continued, and she was cutting in between aisles and racks of clothing. At one point, she didn't know I was near and cut directly in front of me. My plan was to just stop her, but not to hurt her. Just delay her enough for someone to apprehend her. But she turned just in time and ran into a narrower area between two clothing shelf units. At that point, I lost sight of her, so I flew back to the main front aisle, knowing that at some point, she'd have to move back to the front. By this time, the lady whose cries alerted me to the girl's presence had made her way over, and a small crowd was beginning to gather.

"Did she take your wallet too?" the woman asked.

Knowing the truth in my spirit, but still wanting to believe otherwise, I said, "Well, mine is missing, and I can't prove she did it, but I think she did."

Suddenly, the girl shot up the main aisle perpendicular to where we were, making a beeline for the exit door. A few of us simultaneously yelled, "There she goes!" Then, like a bullet, a young man zoomed past all of us. I've never seen someone take off with that urgency. I took off again too, and the lady followed behind as fast as she could. The young girl made it out the door, and a few of us waited just outside the door. A woman there was holding a phone up to her ear, listening intently.

"She took my phone," she said to me and some other people standing with us. "This is my friend's phone I'm using. I dialed my phone to see if I could hear it ring, and I don't know if she meant to or not, but it picked up, and I've been hearing her run."

By now, there was a large group assembled in the door and just outside the door to see what happened. One woman in particular found it awful that this girl had taken my wallet.

"Oh my, now it's horrible that she'd steal from you, in a wheelchair!"

That really hadn't crossed my mind, and it was one of those comments I'd normally have corrected, but considering the circumstances, I let it slide. Then someone shouted that she'd been apprehended. It turned out that a woman in the very first checkout line near the door was an off-duty officer, and she had abandoned her purchase to join the chase. And the young man who flew past me? He was also an off-duty officer, shopping with his wife and baby.

With the pursuit over, there was an instant calming in the atmosphere. We all waited for instructions on what to do next. I think it was the moment that I saw them bring her in the store that it hit me how young she really was—only fourteen years old.

This is just a kid, I thought. And I suddenly found that my heart ached for her. What drove her to do this? I couldn't help but wonder. Eventually, those with missing items were asked to go out to the car where she'd been stopped as she tried to escape. We all were asked to file a report. The law authorities searched the car, and found the lady's wallet. They also found the missing cell phone. They found $30 cash in the girl's pockets. But my wallet was nowhere to be found.

The two ladies, whose property had been located, finished their paperwork and were allowed to leave. I was asked to stay since my wallet was still missing. One policeman and a store manager asked me to take them to the spot where I had felt the tug on my chair, so I did. Then they asked me retrace my steps one more time to be certain it hadn't just fallen somewhere.

While I did that, their plan was to begin reviewing store security footage.

After Mom and I retraced the path of everywhere we'd been in the store, still not finding the wallet, we returned to a waiting area. By this time, I knew with certainty in my spirit that there was a deeper reason I was the one singled out having to wait, and the longer I waited, the more compelled I felt to speak with the girl. I asked one of the officers if I could please have an opportunity to speak with her. He looked at me, somewhat confused, and told me that it wasn't a normal part of protocol to do that. I explained that I did not want to fuss at her, but that I was in ministry and just felt strongly that I had to talk with her. He said he'd see what could be arranged.

A few minutes later, they led the girl out in handcuffs, and took her to the electronics section of the store. The video review had indeed shown her snatching my wallet, escaping from view, and making her way to the back of the store, where it appeared she had thrown it down somewhere. So they took her to have her to show them where she had ditched it. And sure enough, way at the back of the store, behind some boxes, there they found my wallet, minus the $30 cash that had still been in it.

She admitted that the cash found on her was taken from the wallet, and that's all she had wanted. Keep the cash, ditch the wallet. That was actually a relief to me. I never carry a lot of cash on me, so that hadn't bothered me, but I was not looking forward to cancelling cards, getting a new driver's license, getting new insurance cards, and all the other things that are necessary.

When I got my wallet back, I was faced with the final choice of deciding whether to press charges or not. I knew deeply in my spirit that I was not supposed to do so. The girl was already going to face criminal proceedings from the charges pressed by the other two ladies, and during the course of the afternoon, I was told that this same girl had been caught the week before in the same store for the same offense. My charges weren't going to make a huge difference either way. But an opportunity to speak with this young girl? That's where I felt like my impact might be, so again, I asked to see her and the law officers finally ushered me into the holding room and brought her to me. They leaned in close to monitor the conversation.

As she approached, there was a definitive cockiness about her. I'm not sure what she expected, but I could tell my greeting was a shock to her.

"Hey, sweetheart. How are you?"

In that instant, I saw a wall of defense crumble. In Romans 2:4, we are taught that it is the kindness of God that leads us to repentance. I'm certainly not God, but his spirit is alive in me, and in the moment I spoke, I saw that verse become real before my eyes. Where the young girl had been holding her head high with an almost impatient huff, she suddenly lowered her eyes. I wasn't asking her to apologize, nor is an apology a definitive proof of repentance, but the next words out of her mouth were, "I'm sorry I took your wallet."

I asked her if she needed the money and offered to let her keep the $30.

"No, no…I don't need the money."

I asked her what her name is, and while I obviously won't share it here, it made me smile. It had a very significant geographic meaning to me, so I told her it was a beautiful name.

"Has anyone ever told you that you have a destiny?"

Her answer surprised me.

"What does that mean?"

Apparently, no one ever had.

"It means God has a perfect plan for your life. Even your name is full of promise. You can be a voice to the nations, telling people about Jesus."

I had her attention now, or so it seemed.

"Promise me something?" I asked.

"What?"

"Promise me that you won't ever do this again and that the next time I hear your name, it will be for good things…showing that you're walking out that destiny."

"Okay."

"I'm not going to press charges."

"Thank you…" Her voice was barely a whisper.

I knew my job for that moment was done. I didn't feel led to say or do anything more, so I turned and left. No one said a word.

In the years since, I have thought of her often. What court battle did she face? Where is she now? Has she accepted Jesus? At seventeen as of the time of this writing, is she walking out that perfect destiny? I hope someday we cross paths again, because I genuinely care about her and her future. I want to know what she is doing with her life. When she crosses my mind, I smile because I remember a child God loves. An Abba's princess.

I don't have forgiveness perfected, but the Holy Spirit in me does because of what Jesus has done. I've been fully and completely forgiven of all things I've done, and have been fully accepted into his family. So who would I be *not* to forgive?

There are still things that hurt, but hurt is not the same thing as unforgiveness. However, when forgiveness is practiced, hurts are transformed by supernatural healing. Forgiveness is not an unconscious action. It is a deliberate choice. People don't always ask us to forgive them when they've wronged us, but forgiveness of others sets us free too. Furthermore, our choice not to forgive is a choice to become part of someone else's judgment.

> Again Jesus said, "Peace be with you! As the Father has sent me, I am sending you." And with that he breathed on them and said, Receive the Holy Spirit. If you forgive anyone's sins, their sins are forgiven; if you do not forgive them, they are not forgiven.
>
> John 20:21–23 (NIV)

Most people tend to know we aren't supposed to judge, and most have a clear sense of some kind of judgment. But some forms of judgment are more cleverly masked by the enemy. Jesus spoke peace into the disciples, and breathed the Holy Spirit on them. If we believe that the New Testament is still in operation (and we *should*, because it is), then this applies to us as well. We have the same peace of Christ and the same power of his Spirit. So our forgiveness of others releases his peace over them. To withhold forgiveness is to participate in judgment. We are given freedom to enjoy for ourselves, yes. But we are also given freedom for others' sakes.

> It is for freedom that Christ has set us free.
>
> Galatians 5:1 (NIV)

I still have to walk through seasons of forgiving. I also have to ask to be forgiven. But once it became clear to me that unforgiveness is a definite form of judgment, I realized that I don't want to be a part of someone else's judgment. That's not my job. My only main job in life is to worship the Lord because the deeper in his presence I am, the less anything else matters.

From that "place" inside his presence, I've found that I'm insulated from things more, and insulation protects from the pain of the enemy's insults. It's the safest place to be to guard one's heart. That's where I want to live the rest of my existence—both here on earth and in the age to come. And I highly recommend it to everyone reading this book. There is no better place to be than smack dab in the middle of his presence, where you're enveloped in absolute forgiveness, so much so that forgiveness flows out as the pure wellspring of life that can only come from a guarded heart.

Moments of Reflection

1. Have you ever struggled with forgiveness?

2. How does the realization that unforgiveness is a form of judgment change your outlook on forgiveness?

3. How do you *know* you have forgiven?

4. Is offering an apology the same thing as asking for forgiveness? Why or why not?

5. How are you affected when you ask for forgiveness?

Prayer of Refining

Dear Abba, thank you so much for forgiving my own sins through the blood of your son. Make me constantly aware of the ongoing work of forgiveness in my relationships with others. Lord, help me be quick to forgive and quick to ask forgiveness in all circumstances. Show me any areas of unforgiveness that remain in my life. Lord, I repent of them (list each one he brings to mind) and I ask for your grace to walk out this repentance.

In the name of Jesus, so be it. Amen!

Discerning True Humility

When I was around nineteen, I first started really feeling the urge to write. But then I was still very much in bondage in a lot of areas, and with a lack of direction as to how to begin, I knew it just wasn't time. A few years later, when I asked the Lord in prayer what I was born to do, he answered very simply.

"You were born to worship."

That was a very precious gem to me, knowing that the most impacting purpose for my life is just to worship him. It didn't matter where, when or how to him, as long as it was "worship in spirit and truth," as we read about in John 4:24 (NASB).

To me though, I wanted to know my own personal gifting I could use in worship of and service to him. Oh, I've taken spiritual gifts tests and such. I believe those can be good indicators if firmly based in Scripture, but I also believe they can be limitations if they're taken as solid gospel. I've known people, who've taken such tests and get so bogged down in that definition that it's become their only focus, and I believe at that point, they've locked into a human perception of themselves and have stopped relying on his Spirit. I didn't want that locked in definition of myself. So I asked him.

"Lord, what is my gift?"

"Your gift is words."

His answer was simple and clear. There was no doubt in my mind that I'd heard him and it reignited that desire to write. I felt like the ball was in my court, and I was determined to run with it. So for a season, I studied writing and I did a lot of writing. I joined online critique groups, submitted articles, and at one point, even tried writing a Christian suspense novel. I did have a couple of pieces published in some anthologies, but aside from that, it never seemed to go anywhere.

After a while, I started feeling the desire to write waning, and to be honest, that bothered me. If my gift was words, why was writing losing its fun? I realized at that point that this too had become a self-competition based on performance orientation. It had crossed out of words of worship into just words on a page. So I believe the block I was experiencing was to protect my gift of words from spiritual prostitution. From then on, it became a burning passion to completely protect what God had given me to share, and for a while, it was *so* protected that I didn't even write at all. I dropped out of all writing groups and trusted the Lord to guide me and be my teacher. And the day came when he gave me the commission to do what you now hold in your hands.

"Tell your story."

The simple direction was overwhelming. It took a lot of miles and a lot of healing to be able to finally sit and write it. Some of the delay was because of those things, but some of the delay? It was something called false humility, and it was a sobering revelation to finally see that false humility is nothing more than pride in disguise.

To understand the difference between true humility and false humility, we must first have a revelation of what it means to be righteous. For most people, their idea of living a righteous life tends to be trying to do right. There's nothing wrong with wanting to do right and live a holy and set apart life. In fact, we *must* make that a priority in our worship of God and in our daily lives. However, something I've often heard my longtime pastor, Roger Bourgeois, say is that "we aren't human *doings*…we are human *beings*." Doing right things is not what makes us holy and righteous. That's where Jesus comes in. It is his blood that made us to *be* holy and righteous. The doing right things part is the fruit of the ongoing process of sanctification.

With this revelation, we are equipped to see the differences between true and false humility. When we realize on a deep level that it is Jesus and Jesus alone who makes us righteous, and that there is *nothing* we can *do* to save ourselves, we can't help but be humble. I remember the moment this concept gelled for me, and it was in such a mundane circumstance when it happened. God does that to me often. He knows I have that tendency to overthink things, so he waits until I'm in a totally different frame of mind. When my mind is occupied with other things, he can then slip a nugget in and it strikes so deeply to find its mark that I don't have time to think about it first. I call them God's one line zingers. So on this particular day, I was grocery shopping with my mother. We were in the meat department. From a seated position, I'm too short to see the top shelf, so I looked up at the mirror above it to see the reflection of the packages on the top. When I did so, I caught a glimpse of my own wheels. It struck me that I was extremely blessed to be able to shop for groceries with Mom. That's when Abba delivered the zinger.

"You'd still be valuable to me even if you didn't have that chair and couldn't leave the house."

It floored me for a moment, so I literally stopped to let it sink in. Right there in Wal-Mart, the truth of God's unconditional love hit me in a brand new way. If I was born to worship, it doesn't matter where, how or when. It is him and him alone, who gives me value. He is my audience of one. It's not what I do, what I am physically able to accomplish, where I go, or who I know. None of those things defines my value. On the other side of that spectrum, nothing I can't do, what I can't accomplish, where I haven't been or who I don't know...none of those things degrades my value. I have intrinsic worth and value just because the Creator of all things chose to give me worth and value. He deemed me righteous through Christ's blood. As that sunk in, I knew that *not* telling my story was false humility. False humility was backing me into a corner where unintentionally, I was propagating a focus on unworthiness. And focusing on unworthiness is actually a form of glorifying the flesh. Therefore, what I was doing was minimizing the cost of his sacrifice.

God has done so much for me, to set me free and enable me to live victoriously. So I can confidently share my story because it brings him glory.

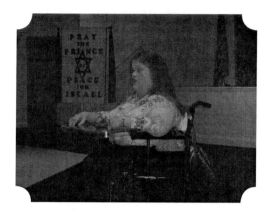

Now, I can confidently share my story because it brings him glory.

True humility means that I *have* to tell the story because it is not for my own benefit, but to worship him, and therefore to propagate his worthiness instead of my unworthiness. But before I could come to that point, I had to realize that my reluctance to share the story of my life was rooted in pride. I was afraid of drawing attention to myself. Like I mentioned in an earlier chapter, I really struggled with self-image issues for most of my life, so attention was not something I wanted. I was afraid people would make fun of me, or think I looked foolish. Those were all clever little lies of the enemy cleverly disguised as humility, but the truth was it was false humility.

Somewhere along the way, I realized that whether I liked it or not, I *do* stand out. Until then, I had been looking at it totally amiss. Until I no longer need a wheelchair or physical help, I will never be able to blend in. I seem to live a life full of shock value. When I came to terms with that, I made a decision. If I am going to stand out either way, I might as well let my standing out take a stand for the kingdom.

There is a song by Cory Asbury called "All Is For Your Glory." I love it for more than one reason, but one part goes, "So catch me up in your story, all my life for your glory." It doesn't say, "all my life after my miracle for your glory." It says simply, "*all* my life for your glory."

For me, this means catching me up in God's story for me now...in the season where I do believe for miracles but haven't yet experienced a miracle enabling me to walk. For this season, this *is* my life, and even it is for his glory.

I love my life, including spending time with Kingdom friends, like Kathy (left) and Laura (right).

It's not about me anyway...now or then. It's only about him. This is my part for now in his story. No one on earth can tell my piece like I can because no one has experienced it quite like I did. No one else can share the same lessons I've learned like I can. And guess what?

No one else can tell your part like you can. No one can impact the world like you can. And no one else can share his faithfulness quite like you can because no one else has your testimony. So don't be afraid to share it. Some people will always see confidence as pride, and some will even go so far as to make accusations that your sharing is self-seeking. However, our responses to those accusations will be the fruit that indicates our motives.

> For in him we live, and move, and have our being; as certain also of your own poets have said, For we are also his offspring.
>
> Acts 17:28 (KJV)

If this verse is truly the revelation we walk in, then we are living our lives *in* him. So if Christ is *love*, and we are truly in him, then we are motivated wholly by love. Love is not self-seeking. So by inference, we can know that pride then is devoid of love. So when we are responding to others from a place of *love*, it will be apparent.

> In God we boast all the day long, and praise thy name forever. Selah.
>
> Psalm 44:8 (KJV)

We have to remember and *rest* in knowing that only God knows the depths of our hearts. Everything else is just external judgment. But God will know. He sees if we are operating from confidence rooted in love, or if we are operating from false humility rooted in pride. And as long as we're confidently boasting in him, that's perfectly acceptable. What we all have to remember is this —we were worth the price Jesus paid for us or he wouldn't have paid it, nor would our Father have allowed him to make such a costly purchase. It all comes down to being grateful for his redemption and being excited about taking our places in his grand and incredible story by letting him flow through the gifts he's given us. We are his reward. So it is a joy to walk confidently in his love.

Moments of Reflection

1. Have you ever experienced the realization that you have held off on doing something due to false humility?

2. How can false humility stall spiritual growth?

3. What are some defining differences between false humility and true humility?

4. How is righteousness connected with humility?

5. How does true humility affect confidence?

Prayer of Refining

Dear Abba, your righteousness is so beautiful. Thank you for the opportunity to shine forth your glory by sharing instead of hiding it in false humility. Lord, show me where I might be displaying pride in disguise. I repent of this pride, God, and ask you to enable me to walk in the true humility that comes through your righteousness.

In the name of Jesus, so be it. Amen!

Walking in Authority

In 2000, I graduated from a master's degree program and within two weeks of my own graduation, I became a college teacher. It all happened so fast that, even now, when I look back, sometimes it still blows my mind. In those days, I was in what I call an "in between" season. Everything I had thought I'd be moving into was placed on hold, and I found myself smack in the middle of doing something I'd never imagined I'd be doing, at least not so soon.

From graduation to my own classroom took less than two weeks.

At only twenty-three, I wasn't really sure what I was getting into. These feelings of uncertainty were compounded by the knowledge that in addition to my traditional college students, I'd also be teaching significant numbers of nontraditional students who were returning to school after years in raising families, other careers, and military deployments. In short, I'd be teaching some people two and three times my age, and it felt exceedingly awkward for me to get used to the realization that I was the one they would be learning from. Even so, it was an exciting time too. For a young woman, it was fun to have an office of my own. It was a challenge to get to be creative in thinking of ways I wanted to positively impact my students' lives. However, when it came right down to carrying out the duties of being a teacher, to be honest, I was at best, clueless, and at worst, downright terrified. I had to learn fast. It was truly a sink or swim season and situation.

The first day of class came. I remember clearly sitting in my office before trekking down to the classroom for the first class. My stomach was churning, my heart was racing, and for a brief moment, I even wished I had said no to the job offer, despite having no clue what I'd have done instead. But I took a few deep breaths and did the only thing I knew to do. I prayed. In part, I was praying for my own nerves to calm, and as I felt God's peace beginning to wash over me, I began praying that my students would be forever impacted.

I rolled down the hall and into my classroom. The room was already pretty full, and I went to the front desk where the instructor's computer was. There was a girl on the front row I recognized, but the odd thing was that I recognized her for having been in a class *with* me, as a fellow classmate, only months before. I asked her to move the chair for me so I could reach the computer, and she said, "That's where the teacher is supposed to sit." I smiled, though I was feeling nervous, and said, "Yes, I know…that's me." It slightly rattled me, and again, doubts of my own authority crept in. I began to wonder if anyone would listen to me. And even more than that, I felt the weight of responsibility for imparting knowledge to those looking me in the eye. These were students who were entrusting this piece of their educational experience into my hands, and I just wasn't sure this was something I was cut out to do.

That first semester, it took every ounce of fortitude I could muster up to learn the ropes and to find my teaching style. At times, I felt like I was nearly killing myself trying to do everything right all the time. This continued beyond my first year, into the second and then the third. I began to experience burnout. I was in my mid-twenties now, and completely exhausted and drained. I don't think anyone at work knew it, but it was hard for me. I know I kept crying out to God, asking him to sustain me, and to reveal to me if I was even on the right path anymore. On many occasions, it seemed like I was at the end of my rope, yet I had no clue of what I'd do otherwise. So I kept going further into this cycle of trying to please people and falling into burnout. I tried to meet every student's requests, tried to answer every question, and tried to never lose my patience. I was staying long past office hours to attempt to work with each student on their own schedules and terms, extending my work times far beyond what I had imagined. Then one day, it hit me.

"Wait a minute. I'm the teacher. I do get to set some of the rules. Why am I wearing myself out? If I don't set some boundaries, it's not like someone else is going to do it for me."

So I began to reorganize how I managed things in my job. I also began realizing the importance of prioritizing. I didn't want to be an authoritarian leader, but neither did I want to spend every waking moment trying to keep up with demands that I was placing on myself. I finally saw that the position of being a teacher itself carried authority from the school. And I began to walk in that authority by changing how I viewed things and did things, so I started feeling pressure lift. Little did I realize at that time what God was doing, but in later years, it was much clearer. He was teaching me how to walk in delegated authority, and he used my job to do it.

Lots of years have passed since that wakeup call. But the realization of what it meant to me has turned out to be a real world analogy, a parable of sorts, for what happens when we realize our authority in the spiritual sense. He uses what some would call secular positions and circumstances to illustrate and reinforce spiritual truths. And then he uses those spiritual truths and revelations at work within us to effect change in the world. This isn't a new concept. It's been going on all throughout history.

One of my favorite Old Testament stories is that of Deborah in Judges 4. I've often wondered about her life, her choices, how she became a prophetess judge in Israel, and even the story of how she met her husband. Not a lot is said in scripture about Lappidoth, Deborah's husband. There's just the mention of his name, which means "torches." Since Barak's name means "lightning," there is even some theological speculation as to whether Lappidoth and Barak were perhaps one and the same man. Some scholars also say that Lappidoth's name is more of an indicator of Deborah's personality, because it could be translated as, "Deborah, woman of a fiery spirit." However, the general consensus is that Lappidoth was a real man, and that he and Barak were two separate men, both of whom had ultimate respect for Deborah.

She was a woman operating, apparently very effectively, in a man's world. She had a real heart for justice and had to be confident in her own prophetic hearing. The Israelites had gone astray yet again, and as a result were living under opposition from Jabin, king of Canaan, and his army commanded by Sisera. Yet, Deborah prophetically knew that God's heart was for the freedom of the Israelites. We aren't told a lot about what specific event prompted her to call for Barak, but obviously something did. But in Judges 5:2 (NIV), we do see something interesting.

> When the princes in Israel take the lead,
> when the people willingly offer themselves—
> praise the Lord!

Deborah's summoning Barak was an act of initiative based on confidence in her authority from God to lead a nation out of captivity. It was about taking the lead and not being afraid to move forward.

Like Deborah, we have authority from God. Married to a man whose name meant "torches," and fighting in battle alongside a man whose name meant "lightning," she had to be confident. Likewise, if we are functioning as the bride, our bridegroom Jesus is a torch, the *light* of the world, and we partner alongside him from whose very throne come peals of thunder and flashes of lightning. We have authority from heaven.

There is both legitimate and illegitimate authority. Authority that is based in justice and grace is legitimate, but authority based in control is illegitimate. One is based on God's love for us and his justice to see us walk in freedom, while the other one is based in control, which really on a basic level equates to a doubt of God's love. In short, one comes from a position of love, but the other comes from a position of fear. True and legitimate authority is always rooted in love and comes from a place of prayer and intimacy in the secret place. When we operate from a position of love, we're typically so convinced of the goodness of God and his love that we don't even have a desire to control. Authentic authority doesn't need to assert itself. It's automatically recognized because of the sheer presences of the One who grants it.

Yet, the enemy knows this and often throws a curve ball that we might not have expected, and he can use even those closest to us to toss the pitch. I remember one night, talking with a friend about counting the cost of walking in the calling. When we get set free, sometimes our freedom threatens others around us. People may have known us as being a certain way. But when we allow God to radically change us, we are no longer content to stay the way we were, so suddenly, we're the same person, yet not the same at all. The more we march to the drumbeat of God's heart, the less the world will understand us. We have to be prepared to handle this.

People no longer know how to react because we don't do things like we used to, we don't say things like we used to, and we don't even have the same spirit about us that we used to. That shocks people, and, sometimes, it makes them uncomfortable because our freedom exposes their bondage.

I remember once listening to a teaching by Kathie Walters, and she said something I will never forget. She said, "Either our bondage will bind people up or our freedom will set others free."

That one statement flew straight to the core of my being, and since then, it's become my own version of Jabez's prayer. Jabez prayed, "Oh, that You would bless me indeed, and enlarge my territory, that Your hand would be with me, and that You would keep me from evil, that I may not cause pain!" (1 Chronicles 4:10 NKJV). So my version of the prayer is something like, "Lord, that you would continually reveal to me the ways of freedom in you, that my own bondage will break off, and that my freedom will be liberating to others."

I'm a work in progress, but that is my prayer.

Moments of Reflection

1. What is your immediate reaction when you find yourself in a position where you are placed "in charge" but don't yet feel equipped?

2. What can you do in those kinds of situations in order to regain your bearings?

3. In what is legitimate authority based?

4. In what is illegitimate authority based?

5. How has your freedom ministered freedom to others?

Prayer of Refining

Dear Abba, thank you for the legitimate authority you've given me as a son or daughter in your kingdom. I want to walk in your freedom to the extent that when others are around me, they are set free also. Lord, the price Jesus paid was too much to waste, so show me ways to use all the benefits that you have given us. Make me continually aware of opportunities to minister freedom in the manner you'd have me do so.

In the name of Jesus, so be it. Amen!

Being Refined and Redefined

When we walk in the freedom of knowing our authority in Christ, it is really a wonderful place of liberty. However, there are labels attached to us throughout life that will need to be submitted to the authority of Jesus. Like I mentioned in the preceding chapter, some of these labels are blatant attacks on self-esteem and confidence in the kingdom, like when people call a Deborah spirit by the name of Jezebel in a case of mistaken identity. However, the enemy uses some labels much more surreptitiously. They're so *logical* that we just accept them and without realizing it, we have accepted those attached definitions of us.

My life has been chock full of labels tossed in my direction, most of them not given with ill-intent at all. They were just words used in a logical fashion that tried to take up residence in my identity. Some had a longer run at sticking around than others, but now, I am vigilant about the labels I accept, both good and bad.

The first vivid memory I have of such a defining label came when I was eleven years old. I was scheduled for extensive spinal surgery to treat scoliosis. During the period of time leading up to the surgery, there was a lot of discussion among a lot of people about my condition, what I was being treated for, and the long-term effects of both the treatment, and the overall diagnosis that even led to scoliosis in the first place. In one such exchange of information, I became aware of the word "terminal" attached to my life. As a curious eleven-year-old who had a voracious appetite for books and knowledge, when I heard that word and didn't know what it meant, the first thing I wanted to do was look it up. I was at school at the time, so I asked a friend to bring me a dictionary and I looked up that intriguing word.

Terminal means ending in death?

That knowledge first made me feel like all the air had been sucked out of my lungs and then it settled like a rock into the pit of my stomach. Anger soon followed. Up until then, I knew that the medical nature of my life was not like other kids, and I knew that doctors had said I'd die before I was three. But hey, at eleven, I figured I was home free. Since I'd long passed that three-year mark, I felt like I was past danger and like I was now just living. I was fully unaware that people were still expecting my death, and now some believed there was a real possibility of its imminence as I faced the very serious spinal fusion just a few weeks ahead. Fear threatened to take root, but the anger I felt was stronger than the fear, and it gave way to a dogged determination. I would live, if it killed me to do so!

The surgery journey wasn't easy. What was intended to be a six to eight hour procedure kept me in the operating room for twelve hours and fifteen minutes. My parents were later told that at one point, my blood pressure became so unstable that I lay there cut open on the operating table while the medical personnel worked diligently to stabilize me and save my life. For two of those over twelve hours, it was very touch and go. But I lived. And about a week later, I went home to recuperate. For thirteen months, I wore a body brace. I spent the first half of my sixth grade year on hospital homebound for school, working hard not to fall behind. Eventually, the brace came off, I returned to school, and I was fully alive.

Other cringe-inducing labels have been assigned to me over the years. Retarded. Crippled. Pitiful. The list goes on. Terminal was just one of many. Not all of them have had negative connotations. There've also been labels like inspirational. Determined. Intelligent. But as surprising as it may be, even the "good" labels must be examined.

When I finally decided to leave the Egypt of my past, all I wanted more than anything else was to be wrapped up in the embrace of God. Stepping out of Egypt headed for the Promised Land meant there was wilderness to traverse, and it didn't take long for me to realize that the purpose of the wilderness is the process. Refiner's fire is hot, and in the kingdom walk, there are increasing degrees of heat intensity. However, the end result is coming out as pure gold, free of dross. For me personally, part of that process meant examining my life and all the labels affixed, not only by others, but by the enemy, by myself, and by the Lord himself. It became crucial for me to know how God labeled me. I wanted only the Lord's labels to remain.

We have to choose which definitions we will identify with. When words are spoken over us, we *must* line them up beside the Word of God to know if they are accurate or not. If they do line up, those labels fit. If they don't line up, then those labels are dross and need to be burned up. For a serious Kingdom Christian, the refinement process never ends until we take our last breath here, and our heart beats the last time. We are living breathing instances of the Refiner's fire at work.

The world will always want to label us…to name us. There are countless Scripture passages linking names to destinies. In several cases, there were literal name changes associated with a person stepping into destiny. One of the most visible and influential changes was Jacob becoming Israel.

> Then Jacob was left alone, and a man wrestled with him until daybreak. When he saw that he had not prevailed against him, he touched the socket of his thigh; so the socket of Jacob's thigh was dislocated while he wrestled with him. Then he said, "Let me go, for the dawn is breaking." But he said, "I will not let you go unless you bless me." So he said to him, "What is your name?" And he said, "Jacob." He said, "Your name shall no longer be Jacob, but Israel; for you have striven with God and with men and have prevailed." Then Jacob asked him and said, "Please tell me your name." But he said, "Why is it that you ask my name?" And he blessed him there. So Jacob named the place Peniel, for he said, "I have seen God face to face, yet my life has been preserved."
>
> Genesis 32: 24–30 (NASB)

A huge part of refinement is redefinition. The world labels us and has its Babylonian expectations for us. Those labels are always coupled with corresponding expectations. So to walk in absolute freedom, we *must* know what the Word says about us. Then we must *un*define what the world has said and then take on the labels that God has given us. We must reject all Babylonian expectations and ascribe to kingdom of heaven expectations. By doing so, we undergo what appears to be serious redefinition.

However, something I also have discovered is that redefinition is often really just deliverance in action. As we get delivered from things, including labels, the process is akin to uncovering gemstones in a field of dirt. As one layer of dirt at a time is stripped away, more and more of the underlying beauty is revealed. It doesn't change the fact that there was a ruby or sapphire or emerald there all along. It's just that somewhere along the way, a unique treasure was dropped into the dust, and then subsequently covered by years' worth of grime. God *always* saw the brilliance. It was always there, shining underneath the muck and mire. It's just that the world had obscured the truth of the treasure's identity. So during the "cleanup" process, a pile of dirt doesn't *become* a gemstone. The ruby was always a ruby. The sapphire was always a sapphire. The emerald was always an emerald. They just get uncovered.

In Jacob's case, he had reached a point where facing God was more favorable than facing the labels associated with his past. He had succumbed to the expectations of those labels in previous years when he deceived his brother. But after trials and growth, he finally reached that place where the pain of change was more pleasant than the pain of staying the same. Our struggle for redefinition rarely happens in the open surrounded by people. Instead, like Jacob, redefinition of our identity happens when we are "left alone" with God. It sounds cliché, but there is some real truth in reaching that place of "being sick and tired of being sick and tired."

As we realize that labels placed on our lives really are *not* what God has said of us, we begin to have a growing desire for the manifestation of what he *has* said of us. The hunger for that destiny compels us to move out of the trap of labeled expectations. When we get sick enough of *wanting to* be what God has said, we finally realize we have the courage to actually walk in that identity. Then, the boldness arises in us to meet God in our own personal equivalent of Peniel, where we receive both identity in him and the blessings that come with it. But perhaps the most interesting part of all of this kind of journey lies in the arising boldness.

That kind of boldness is born of the desire to know his identity for us. But the root of this desire even is in God's grace. Jesus said, "No one can come to Me unless the Father who sent Me draws him" (John 6:44, NASB). What we can infer from this is that God himself wants us to come to Christ and to know who we are in him so strongly that he will draw us to him. We *think* it is our hunger drawing us to him, but it is really *him* drawing us to himself. Hunger for his expectations is just the tool he uses.

When I reached that point of desiring God's expectations for me, nothing else mattered. Seeking him more and more led to an amazing discovery. I discovered that our adherence to his identity for us results in blessings for others too. He will reveal himself to others and then will reveal their own identities to them.

> I will give you the treasures of darkness
> And hidden wealth of secret places,
> So that you may know that it is I,
> The Lord, the God of Israel, who calls you by
> your name.
> For the sake of Jacob My servant,
> And Israel My chosen one,
> I have also called you by your name;
> I have given you a title of honor
> Though you have not known me.
>
> Isaiah 45:3–4 (NASB)

God blessed Cyrus to bless Israel. He still does that today. He blesses people to bless us, even when those people haven't known him. When you have favor with God, you will have favor with men. For reasons they can't understand, they will be compelled to bless you. Likewise, he blesses us to bless others. We are to give as freely as we have received.

> Heal the sick, raise the dead, cleanse those who
> have leprosy, drive out demons. Freely you have
> received; freely give.
>
> Matthew 10:8 (NIV)

So with freedom comes the responsibility to use it. It is indeed meant to be enjoyed, but it is also meant to be shared.

Jacob's willingness to take his previous labels and expectations directly to God resulted in the birth of a nation. Thousands of years later, people don't talk about the tribes of Jacob. They talk about the tribes of Israel. Jacob isn't the nation the whole world watches. Israel is. With redefinition comes blessing and unlocked destiny.

God is my definer and refiner. I've found that when I take a Velcro mentality to his identity for me and a duck's back mentality to the world's identity for me, his promises stick with me, and the world's demands slide right off. I experience a level of peace that surpasses understanding, which makes me free to walk in the plans he alone can script for me. I know who I am, and I know who I'm not, so when new labels head my way, I know where to go to see if the process of refinement reveals them to be gold or dross.

Moments of Reflection

1. What labels in your life line up appropriately with the word of God?

2. What labels in your life do not line up appropriately with the word of God?

3. What are some of the ways you have "gone through the process" in your own wilderness seasons?

4. Even your wilderness seasons have purpose. How does knowing this change how you view those seasons?

5. What scriptures have the most meaning to you regarding refining and redefining?

Prayer of Refining

Dear Abba, you have called me yours. That's all that matters. The labels that the world would place on me can never compare to being yours. Even the good things people say I am are pale in comparison to your glory and majesty. Help me to identify the labels that do not line up with your word, and then set me free from those. Help me to identify the labels that do line up with your word, and build those into my spirit as you would have them remain. Above all, Lord, just remind me of the simplicity of just resting in who you say I am.

In the name of Jesus, so be it. Amen!

Aligning for the "New Thing"

When the heat from the process of refinement gets hotter, we often find ourselves in a place of discomfort. But it is what I like to call "holy restlessness" or "divine discomfort." There is such a thing as being out of God's rest, but that's not what I mean in this case.

Holy restlessness is the effect of growth. It is the indicator that where we used to be isn't where we belong anymore, and it provokes us to change. It makes us ready to take the next step, whatever that happens to be in any given set of circumstances. Sometimes the purpose of the next step is to birth something, but sometimes it is to let something die. Sometimes the next step leads to a flurry of activity, but sometimes it is simply a declaration of agreement with the promises of God. I've found myself in all of these circumstances.

The alignment lesson was perhaps one of the most painful ones I've learned. When we consistently align ourselves only with the people who were in the proverbial Egypt with us and really liked it there, we will be held back from moving toward the Promised Land of whatever God has planned for us. In order to change, we have to allow him to change even our environment. Some people will never accept your freedom and your ability to walk in his authority. As a result, they will leave your life, and in some cases, may even attempt to slander your authority. I've had many people cross paths with me, only to extricate themselves from my life when we reached a point where bondage and freedom clashed.

To be fair, I've also left people's lives for the same reasons. I have had moments of weakness where my own bondage was threatened by another's freedom, and I've walked away. But those moments have provoked me to repentance and to seek healing and forgiveness. Being human flesh, either side of the coin can hurt, but we must choose to let it stop us or keep moving forward in faith continually made tender by the things we face.

There was a season in my life where I wondered why I always felt drained from the relationships in my life. I remember finally praying for God to do whatever he had to do to bring me into the place he wanted me. That's a dangerous prayer if you're afraid of change, but it is a safe prayer if you believe God is who he says. So I even asked him to remove all people from my life who weren't the right ones to be in my life. I also asked him to bring new people—*his* choice of friends and relationships into my life.

In the season that followed, one by one I saw practically every previous close friend either move, get married, or just simply drop out of my circle. For some of them, I recognized a need for me to be the one to walk away. So for a tough couple of years, I felt terribly alone. Yet I was growing closer to God than I ever had been. It was a huge part of that redefinition and refining process that I mentioned earlier.

In a friend's wedding on Y2K, January 1, 2000.

If we are truly walking in the transformation of Christ, "we all, with unveiled face, beholding as in a mirror the glory of the Lord, are being transformed into the same image from glory to glory, just as from the Lord, the Spirit" (2 Corinthians 3:18 NASB). That also means from healthy relationship to healthy relationship. When people choose to leave our lives, that is their choice. Glory and darkness cannot coexist. Likewise, freedom and bondage cannot coexist. One will always trump the other. So if our freedom threatens another's bondage, one of two things will happen. The other will get free or they will leave our life to live comfortably in their bondage. Some will be so unable to accept the delivered you that they take it a step further and move into accusation and condemnation, slapping labels on you. As mentioned in a previous chapter, Deborah spirits throughout history have been unjustly called Jezebel spirits, but if this happens, the Lord himself will vindicate. In all cases, I encourage taking the high road, letting the Lord show himself strong and validate his authority at work in your life. He is perfectly capable of defending himself and he is perfectly capable of defending you.

It doesn't mean it won't hurt because honestly, it probably will. So that's where we go back to forgiveness. In Romans 12:18 (AMP), we are instructed to, "if it is possible, as far as it depends on you, live at peace with everyone." When someone else refuses, it's no longer in the "as far as it depends on you" place. So we cannot and should not try to control another's reaction to our freedom. We should then pray, forgive, let go, and step ahead. Let God have it. It's very possible that he is allowing it for the greater purpose of aligning you for destiny.

From left to right behind me, Heidi Hunter, Kathy Milsap, and Jerry Hunter, three of the friends God brought into my life.

As I grew in that season myself, I found something interesting happening. One by one, a variety of new individuals started coming into my life. It was not an overnight thing. It took time, but over another couple of years, I began realizing that the people to whom God was introducing me were people who spoke into my life, uplifted me, challenged me, and overall, had similar goals and priorities, all of which centered around God and kingdom. And all I had to do was ask him to reorder my friendships. I've been so blessed.

When I received the baptism of the Holy Spirit in the summer of 2007, I knew something had changed. I had turned a corner, and it was now clearer than ever to me that committing to a lifetime of ministry was God's plan for me. There's a popular colloquial saying that most people know. "Fish or cut bait." Here in the South, there's also a much more colorful and blunt colloquialism meaning the same thing, and that most people know, but I won't quote that one! Both, however, essentially mean, "Make a decision. If you're going to do something, do it. If not, forget it."

I had reached that point. For years, I had felt God calling me, and, now, I even had an amazing circle of friends and mentors who were in my corner, but I had not yet fully committed to it. I, however, knew that it was time to either get serious or get out. Be a dreamer only or actually *do* the things I dreamed about. So I finally said yes, and from that point onward, it felt like finally the Holy Spirit was in the driver's seat and had his foot with the pedal to the metal.

I was still carrying plenty of wounds and hurts from my past, but I could literally feel them leaving. As those hurts got healed, those places were replaced with new life and new dreams, as well as with the resurrection of some old dreams I had almost forgotten. In other cases, it wasn't as much about healing as it was about taking a stand. In the past, I'd have ignored things or just accepted things even if they were wrong or unjust. But the growing boldness enabled me to finally speak out. I'd find myself praying in the Spirit, and as I did, I could feel the acceleration in my own spirit.

For a few years, I had dropped out of attending church. I had still prayed, read the Bible, and I'd even say I had still grown. But at some point in the fall of 2007, I knew I couldn't continue to grow alone locally. I really desired a local church family to fellowship with on a regular basis. So on December that year, at God's prompting, I returned to the church I had most recently attended regularly several years prior. From the moment I returned, I knew it was the right decision. I knew the next step would soon follow, but I wasn't quite sure what it would be just yet.

In the spring and summer of 2008, the Florida Healing Outpouring was going on in Lakeland, Florida, and every evening, I found myself glued to the livestream on GodTV. For hours, I'd soak in worship, and I'd see testimonies that took my breath away. Deep inside my spirit, I ached to be able to go, but I wasn't in a position to be able to at the time. I also wanted to know someone from that area who was involved personally in seeing how it was changing that region. When the events surrounding the end of that main move began happening, I was as sad to see it as anyone. In the weeks and months after it, some people were intent on invalidating the entire thing on the basis of one leader's moral downfall, declaring that the entire outpouring wasn't even a legitimate move of God. However, all I knew was that something in me had been ignited. Regardless of what had happened with the individuals involved, I had seen past humanity and received a glimpse of the power of God. He had used that season to build my faith in a way that no other season prior to it had.

During the latter part of the previous year, my friend Scott had introduced me to the music of Judy Jacobs. I wasn't really familiar with her at all before that, but the first time I heard her sing one of my all-time favorite songs, "Days of Elijah," I knew I wanted to know more about her. At that point, I had no idea that she had a powerful ministry of which music was only one part. I remembered clearly the moment I discovered that she had a ministry mentoring institute, and as I watched the introductory video, I knew this was the next step I had been waiting for. I saw that the ministry location wasn't terribly far from me, so even though I had missed that year's event, I knew in my heart that I'd be attending the next one. But in the waiting, I had a deep desire to meet this woman. I wanted to know for sure that this was the right direction, and I asked the Lord to confirm it. He did so in a manner so clear that I'd have been a fool to ignore it.

One Sunday afternoon in late December 2007, my family and I were riding through our town on our way to do some Christmas shopping in a nearby town. This was a road we didn't travel on a lot, but as we did on that day, I saw a church marquee sign and exclaimed,

"Oh my gosh!" I think I made everyone in the van jump. The sign declared that soon after the first of the year, Judy Jacobs was coming to *my* town, which isn't a big town at all. I quickly made a note of the date, and eagerly anticipated it. I knew this was God giving me the opportunity to hear this woman and meet her.

When the weekend of her visit drew near, much to my disappointment, it snowed. Here in the South, it doesn't snow enough to disrupt events very often, but on this occasion it was just enough ice and snow to change plans. As a result, her visit was postponed. It had been something I looked forward to, and when the snow came, I wondered if I'd have another opportunity. Only a few weeks later, I found out.

My mother's friend from high school attended the church that was going to host Minister Judy, and she called my mom to tell her that the event had been rescheduled. When I found that out, I was ecstatic, but it was *when* it was to be held that reignited my level of expectation. The new date was the weekend before my birthday. To this day, I remain firmly convinced that the date change was especially for confirmation that I *was* hearing God, but more importantly, it was to remind me that he was hearing me. I did indeed meet Minister Judy that day and felt certain that things were accelerating even more.

It was October of that year when I attended my first mentoring main event in Cleveland, Tennessee, and to be honest, I was at first more than a little intimidated. I was downright shaking in my socks at times. Every minister out of the panel of speakers, singers, mentors and staff that served with the event and the International Institute of Mentoring functioned with a boldness and zeal that I had been longing to see manifested in me. To my delight, one of the ministers, Apostle Shirley Arnold, who has now become another strong ministry influence in my life, pastored a church in Lakeland, Florida. One of the nights, as she spoke, she mentioned that no matter what had happened at the end of the healing outpouring, revival was alive and well in Lakeland.

I was thrilled to meet someone who'd been in the area and who was seeing the lasting effects, so even that was an answer to prayer. Throughout the entire mentoring main event weekend, I had never experienced in person such powerful conviction and commitment to advance the kingdom of God by so many people at the same time. In smaller groups, yes, but suddenly, here I was, surrounded with hundreds of other people who had also responded to God's call to take a step of faith into the unknown. It was incredible. And it felt so...*right*.

After the IIOM main event, I came back home, full of faith and fire, and determined to find my place. In less than a year's time, I had become aligned with a church home and with a powerful international ministry, both of which were right on target with what I had been seeking.

In both cases, interestingly enough, the alignment was something only God could have orchestrated. When we, as individuals, try to make things happen, it's a process of strife. But during this entire season of alignment for me, all I really did was keep myself in the presence of God. I didn't have a clue what else to do, so I just sought his face. It was the Lord who did all of the aligning, prompting me to do this or that, and giving me opportunities to engage with his plans. I just accepted his invitations, for lack of a better way to describe it.

When there is a mandate on our lives, proper alignment is crucial. But what we have to remember is this—that mandate is God's plan, and he is fully equipped to get us into position to meet the people we need to meet, and to introduce us into the places we need to be to fulfill that mandate. Yes, at some point, we will have to take action, but what we have to do first is get into proper position before the face of God. From that point on, he will orchestrate the divine appointments.

Moments of Reflection

1. What has been the response of those around you when you began to walk in a new level of faith?

2. How have you responded?

3. What has been your biggest struggle in "leaving Egypt for the Promised Land"?

4. Can you look back now and see, at least in part, how God has been realigning your life?

5. If you have never asked the Lord to reorder your life and relationships, are you ready now?

Prayer of Refining

Dear Abba, you know who you've made me to be. You know your plans for my life. So I acknowledge and embrace that this means you know everyone and every circumstance that must leave or enter my life to bring those plans to fulfillment. Lord, I ask you to reorder my life and relationships as necessary to walk in fullness. I am fully aware that this may mean changes, some of which may be difficult. Even so, Father, I give you permission because I know that my heart and destiny are safest in your hands.

In the name of Jesus, so be it. Amen!

Becoming a Body in Motion

As the Lord begins to align our lives, that alignment has an interesting effect—it makes us begin to take steps we never could before. He has to get us into the right "places" with the right influences, and then if we're truly in acceptance of his purposes and plans, we will begin to shift into motion.

Sometimes we think God is making us wait, when in reality, he is waiting on us. We have to begin changing first. Then when we've finally said yes to him, those alignments he makes produce change in our lives.

In the field of mechanics, Isaac Newton's laws of motion are the foundation upon which many other principles are based. They laid the groundwork for understanding how things work in the physical world. And for years, I've said that those same laws are equally as applicable to the spiritual world as they are to the physical world.

Newton's first law of motion is that an object at rest remains at rest unless another force acts upon it, and an object in motion remains in motion at its same velocity, also unless another force acts upon it. In our lives, we tend to conform to these laws too. If we are just sitting still spiritually, we will not see God's promises in action. But the Holy Spirit is a powerful force, competent and able to be the force that acts upon us, propelling us into motion.

For me, when I surrendered and allowed him to set me into motion, he started by challenging my old mindsets and getting me out of my comfort zone. In fact, he *still* does this and always will. I knew he was calling me into a place of radical faith for a lot of things, including healing. One night in late summer of 2008, I was thinking about major moves of the Holy Spirit and was drawn to study some past revivalists. That night, as I read about Smith Wigglesworth and his bold and often unconventional methods, I read a miracle story about him telling a man who had no need for shoes to go buy a pair. When the man did it, he received a phenomenally creative miracle. As I read this account, I heard the Lord speak to me.

"I want *you* to buy a pair of faith shoes."

It was so sudden that it startled me. My analytical practicality tried to shove off the "thought," but when he said it again, I knew it wasn't just me thinking. I don't intentionally just think uncomfortable thoughts, and this was so uncomfortably out of my comfort zone that it was a challenge. It was the Lord and this was to be an act of faith. I hadn't been able to wear shoes since I was ten or eleven, and honestly, as a female, I missed it a lot. I love shoes, and can't help but notice them on other people. It's not a sad longing thing. As any woman can vouch, it's just a woman thing. But when the Lord impressed upon me to buy shoes, I felt kind of silly.

"Lord, people will think I'm nuts. Worse yet, they'll feel sorry for me. Besides, I don't even know what size shoes I'd buy since I've never worn shoes as an adult."

Still, his words penetrated my doubts, and finally I responded, "Okay, Lord. I'll do it. But what shoes and what size?"

It's hard to explain but I felt him smile.

"Just look for the perfect pair. You'll know them when you see them. Size 6 ½."

My "Holly" faith shoes arrived in time for Christmas 2009.

I knew that if I was going to buy shoes, I wanted *shoes*, which was something that was worth waiting for. Something that was so "me" that I'd know they were truly the perfect shoes. I began browsing, looking for shoes online and I looked in stores. Sometimes, something would momentarily catch my eye, but nothing captured my gaze completely. Over the next few weeks and months, I'm sure I must've looked at hundreds of pairs of shoes. Finally one evening, I found them online. The photo captured my attention first. They were silver high heels, blingy, and perfect for dancing. So I clicked on the thumbnail photo to display the item name and description. That's when the tears began to fall. The style name of that particular shoe was "Holly." Not only had I found the perfect pair of shoes, but they literally had my name assigned to them. Again, I felt God smile. In retrospect, I should've bought the shoes right there on the spot, but they were an expensive item, and it still took some time to let my brain wrap around the concept. But I held onto them in my heart. Finally, just before Christmas in 2009, I was praying again about this act of faith, and the Lord lovingly, yet playfully, said to my spirit, "Just buy the shoes already."

Christmas with family. On the left, me with my sister-in-law (with Conner in back). In the center, me with my brother (with Chloe hanging on behind). On the right, me with my niece.

So I went back online to buy the shoes, and interestingly, when I did, they were on sale and came with free shipping. Even in my slowness to respond, God still blessed me. I still haven't been able to wear them, but guess what? I've never for one second regretted buying them. I own them, I know they are a gift from God, and I know they are a reminder of his promises. He cared enough to even have my name on them. He's definitely into details.

That experience taught me that he will often ask us to do things we've never done. That can be hard if we are locked into mindsets that tell us not to do things that don't make sense. When we get into routines and rituals, it can be difficult to change. We can begin to stagnate in life overall, and in our spiritual life, if we do not commit to remain in motion. I'm definitely not a proponent of religious activity just for the sake of doing something and anyone who knows me well can attest to that fact. A lot of religious activity can still be stagnation. So that's not what I mean here. What I mean is that in order to continue growing, we must commit to *begin* somewhere. It is a personal thing. We have to become a "body in motion" spiritually speaking by yielding to the Holy Spirit to set us into motion. If we don't, we stagnate.

Newton's second law of motion is that a body's acceleration is in direct proportion to and in the same direction as the force acting on a body, and in inverse proportion to its mass. If we are truly sold out to and committed to advancing the kingdom of God, then when his force hits us to propel us, we will—it's not that we may—we *will* accelerate in direct proportion to his will. For some, it will seem to take longer, whereas for others, it will appear to be rapid acceleration. The difference is in the mass we carry.

If we have a lot of extra baggage, we tend to accelerate slower. And baggage can mean a lot of things. It can mean oppression, pain and wounding from which we need deliverance and inner healing. In those cases, as those burdens and weights break off of us, we become lighter and lighter in the spirit; and thus we will be able to accelerate faster. The sooner we choose to undergo that inner healing, the sooner we find ourselves in the acceleration process. Even that is a choice. Some people have a very difficult time letting go of things, simply because even though they're painful, at least they're familiar. But the sooner we choose to let the chains fall off, the sooner we will find ourselves in motion.

Baggage can also mean spiritual bloat as well. A disturbing trend I've seen in the American church for years has been a consumption of knowledge with little usage. So people sit in churches or under a variety of teaching, going from buffet to buffet (or conference to conference) gorging on spiritual food, yet not doing anything with it. They become spiritually fat and bloated, full of knowledge, yet lacking in the power to put it into action. Such spiritual bloat causes people to have a convoluted picture of the gospel. The sooner we realize that the Gospel of Jesus Christ is very simple, the faster we can accelerate. It's not that we shouldn't attain knowledge. We most definitely should.

> Be diligent to present yourself approved to God as a workman who does not need to be ashamed, accurately handling the word of truth.
>
> 2 Timothy 2:15 (NASB)

It's only in obtaining knowledge that we can accurately handle the word of truth. But to get into motion, what it takes is the pure and simple gospel. All of the rest will follow. Losing the mass of puffed up religion will lead to accelerated growth. I once heard Apostle Shirley Arnold talking about the kingdom life.

She said, "It's simple. It's not easy, but it's simple."

And she is exactly right. When we just believe, it's simple. It's not that we won't experience other forces at work to attempt to slow us down, because honestly, we will. Actually, that's Newton's third law of motion. When one body exerts a force on another body, the second body will basically push back with a force in the opposite direction of the first body. In other words, if the Holy Spirit propels you forward, the enemy will try to push you back. That opposing force may come through a variety of tools. It could be through circumstances, disagreements, illnesses, and the list goes on.

But more often than not, the resistant force behind them all is the enemy. The important thing to remember is that the force of God is forever more powerful than the force of the enemy. One of the enemy's favorite tools is deception by magnifying his appearance. Most people have a mental picture of something like a continuum of force ranging from good with God on that end to bad with Satan on that end. But that isn't true. Satan is not even on the same continuum. The amount of force he can exert is nowhere near the strength of the Father. In other words, Satan can never be as bad as God can be good.

When we are in alignment according to God's purposes and accelerating according to his plan, we will find more fulfillment than we ever even dreamed possible. It's funny too because sometimes, the fulfillment comes in ways that we never imagined. Things we used to hate doing will become preferable.

We will see things with new eyes. We will approach perceived obstacles through motivation from a renewed mind. It does take submission to the force of change. It also takes a commitment to let go of all the mass that isn't purely from the word of God, and let him alone be the force that accelerates you. But by his grace, with our cooperation, it is not only possible. It is a guarantee.

Moments of Reflection

1. What are some of the steps of faith God has asked you to take in your own life?

2. Reflect on the things you are currently doing "for God" or "for the kingdom." Are any of those things now recognizable as "spiritual bloat"?

3. What are some ways you can release those activities in order to be free to do the ones God has specifically called *you* to do?

4. What are those things you *know* God has called you to do?

5. Are you supposed to wait or is God waiting for you to take a step in that direction?

Prayer of Refining

Dear Abba, I ask that you would set me in motion in whatever manner I need to be mobilized. I want my life to make maximum impact in kingdom advancement, but I cannot do it under my own power. I repent for any spiritual bloat, where I have stepped into my own efforts instead of trusting you. And, Lord, I rest in your power, trusting that you will show me what to do and when to do it. Thank you for the power of your Holy Spirit.

In the name of Jesus, so be it. Amen!

Taking One Step at a Time

Once set into motion, wrapped up in the acceleration process, things can seem to happen quickly. For me, when I got serious, things moved fast…for a while. Only a few months after attending my first mentoring institute, and having a renewed confidence that this dream of mine to reach the nations wasn't just a pipe dream, I realized God had already given me the next steps. I just had to reach a point where I was able to see them. It took putting together a lot of little pieces to see the way the bigger picture was shaping up.

Sometime in that season of next steps, my friend, Carol, sent me a card. It was a simple, sweet thank you note for something, but on the outside was a caption that hit its mark.

"Some dreams come a size too big so we can grow into them."

That's how Deep Calls to Deep Ministries was birthed. It was a dream, and it was way out of my league.

I've long had a heart for people of other cultures and nations. Here in America, quite frankly, we are spoiled. We have everything anyone could ever want and limitless opportunities, yet so many people aren't fulfilled. This is in stark contrast to the extreme poverty, yet abundant joy I see at work in other nations who have such hope when they realize how much God loves them. It's such a different paradigm. So for years, my heart has been to bring the *light* of Jesus wherever people haven't yet met him in whatever ways God leads. I began to feel my heartstrings tugged especially toward the people of India, and this honestly puzzled me because I'd never really had that particular calling before. But I asked the Lord to confirm it. He did so in some incredible ways.

The first most obvious confirmation came while at the IIOM that first time. The entire experience was life-changing, but I found myself praying a lot during it, asking him for direction. On the last day, we were in a sanctuary with a baptismal pool. This part of the schedule was different from the original plan, but since we ended up being in that location, the leaders decided to make use of it by offering baptism to the attendees. Due to the obvious issues with immersion baptism in my case, I'd never experienced that. On more than one occasion, I had started to pursue it, but each time, I'd chicken out and not go through with it. So when that sudden opportunity arose, I felt a burning desire to do it this time. I rather timidly approached one of the IIOM ministry's staff, and asked how I could do it. They discussed it, and asked me a few questions about the electronics on my chair. Finally, we just decided to improvise. We were all in agreement that baptism is a symbolic gesture of being raised to new life in Christ, and we knew that he knew our hearts.

When my turn came, we took lots of spare towels and wrapped up the electronic gadgetry. I rolled up beside the baptismal pool. Apostle Shirley Arnold was standing in the pool along with Minister Judy and her husband, Pastor Jamie. Shirley came forward and asked me several questions regarding my declaration of faith and my commitment to fulfill my call. Finally, it was time, and she said something I will never forget. I may not recall the words exactly, but it was something like this.

"When I go to India, we don't always have a lot of deep water we can baptize in. So we kind of have to splash, and God honors it. I have no problem doing it this way! So, I'm baptizing you like we do it in India."

My baptism at IIOM in October 2008

Until that weekend, she had never met me. She knew absolutely nothing about my interest in India. And while I might be mistaken, I think I'm the only person to whom she made that kind of India-specific statement. That was powerful to me, and positively impossible to ignore. I think it was at that point that I finally surrendered and said, "Okay, Lord. So we begin with India."

That was in October 2008. In February 2009, I attended a conference hosted by Kathie Walters in Marietta, Georgia. I had previously done some computer work for her, but had never met her face to face. So as a birthday present to myself, I decided to go. At that conference, I met a woman from India with a ministry there, and to this day, she is one of the most incredible women I know. For her protection, I don't mention her name here, but I will say this. She has a heart and a fire about her that is contagious. There is a determination in her that is born of adversity that one can only develop after undergoing persecution unlike anything we've seen here in America. I instantly felt a connection deep in my spirit. It was clear to me, and later I found out, clear to her too that it was a kingdom connection. I still wasn't totally sure what to do, but I knew I was to stay in touch with her. So we e-mailed a lot, and I kept seeking the Lord as to how to help.

My sweet sister from India, and Carol, my friend from Ohio, are two more blessings God sent into my life.

God speaks to me often in night dreams. So before I ever attended the IIOM or got involved with a church family, God had been giving me really detailed dreams. Several of them involved rain, water, and waterfalls. Being from the north Georgia mountains area, I grew up loving the terrain, including our creeks and rivers, and especially our waterfalls. It wasn't necessarily that I could get very near to most of them, since most trails weren't very accessible for people on wheels. But some of my entire life's fondest memories revolve around the day-long road trips my family and I would take through the mountains. I was always captivated as the road paralleled the rivers and as cascading waterfalls splashed into view on these treks. It was and still is beautiful. However, I had never really dreamed much about them, and when God started giving me these dreams, I knew it meant something. It just wasn't clear yet what. So I documented those dreams and kept living, waiting for the revelation.

Somewhere around the same time, I sat in church one Sunday morning, with my eyes closed in worship. I started smelling a tropical floral scent. I opened my eyes to look around, and no one was very near me, so I realized this was a different kind of experience. I closed my eyes again and started to pray and ask the Lord about it, but even as my mind was forming the question, he answered.

"What you are smelling is hibiscus."

Since I don't garden, at that moment, I couldn't even remember what a hibiscus looked like. However, I tried to picture it, and was thinking it was a little brushy blue flower, which I later found out was hyacinth. The Lord said, "No."

Instantly, he started showing me a vision. In it, my hands were cupped in front of me, and a big, bright, reddish-coral bloom began to unfold in my hands. It was stunningly beautiful and vibrant. The scent was soft, not overpowering, yet unlike anything I'd ever smelled before or since. But what struck me more than anything was the holiness of the moment. I wanted to ask him a barrage of questions as to what the experience was about, but the moment was so peaceful that the questions faded away and I just enjoyed it.

A couple of days later, I was browsing online, and found myself thinking about the significance of the hibiscus. I also wanted to know what it *actually* looked like. When I did a search for it, my mouth dropped open as I saw photos of red hibiscus flowers that looked very similar to what I had seen in that vision. I found one that looked as close to what I had seen and clicked on it. As I read the caption, tears flooded my eyes again. That specific photo had been taken in India.

Several more similar things happened, but all continued to confirm that I was in motion, albeit one step at a time. These confirmations were road signs, each coming at a point when I wasn't sure if I was still on the right road or if I had somehow gotten off the path. His faithfulness continued to sustain me and raise my own level of faith.

One evening, I was praying and thinking about these signs and about all the waterfall dreams I'd been having. Even though I now was confident I was squarely in God's will, I was experiencing deeper and deeper longings just to know more of him. I wanted to serve him and, on the one hand, it was obvious that he was very near. However, at times, I just didn't feel like I could get close enough. So on this particular evening, I opened my Bible and was reading Psalm 42 when I finally knew what he was saying.

> Deep calls to deep at the sound of Your waterfalls;
> All Your breakers and Your waves have rolled over me.
>
> Psalm 42:7 (NASB)

In that moment, Deep Calls to Deep Ministries was born. It was to be a ministry bringing *hope* to the nations, beginning with India.

In the hospitality room at DCTD's first Confluence conference, from left to right: Roger Bourgeois, Elaine Czaplinski, Scott Cooper, Judy Jacobs, me, Tara Aguirre, Beth Bourgeois, Mary Snow, Carol Vail.

The months that followed were a whirlwind. I had to learn quickly how to go about setting up an official organization underneath the umbrella of my church. I also got more specific in my e-mails to my friend in India, as I investigated ways to be involved in helping her ministry. Every step of everything we've put our hands to has been directed by the Holy Spirit.

None of it happened overnight. It was a process, and I was *really* in a learning curve. But during that season, I learned the truth of Psalm 119:105 (KJV), "Thy word is a lamp unto my feet, and a light unto my path."

There was light for each single step. I couldn't see the whole route, and I still can't until this day. But it's okay. All I need is light for each step. What I've learned also is that it's very important to enjoy the journey. So many people in life get so anxious to reach a destination that they miss the scenery on the route to get there. It's the journey that really makes the experience. And it's also important to remember the significance of timing. Sometimes, it isn't just us that are being prepared.

Psalm 119:105

God is magnificently at work in our lives, but he's also magnificently at work in others' lives, preparing us and preparing them. He's setting up all the future appointments and circumstances that will lead to the fulfillment of his divine plan. So we have to find peace and contentment in the one step at a time process. We may look at a circumstance and see no possible way something can be done. In some of those circumstances, it's just simply that it isn't time yet. For example, when I was a child, wanting to meander close to those north Georgia creeks, rivers, and waterfalls, there were no accessible trails. Now, there is a paved trail that allows access to the beautiful Amicalola Falls. There is a picnic area right off the Toccoa River. While it isn't in the mountains, there is even an almost one hundred mile trail that runs from Smyrna, Georgia, to Anniston, Alabama, which I actually intend to stroll at some point in my future. There are paved trails in lots of places now where before, I could only dream of experiencing the beauty of God's creation. It was just a matter of timing.

That is how God works. He first captures our heart with his love and grace. Then he allows us to experience the refinement process, burning out all the things in us that would hinder us from walking into his destiny for us. Then once we're set into motion, he allows to take one step at a time, learning to trust him at all costs. In every part of the process, he reveals more and more of his nature and character. The deep in him and the deep in us cry out to each other, overtaking us with his majesty. Each step will become clear in exactly the right time. That's how the rest of the future of my own ministry will be. I still don't know how some of the details will work out, but I don't have to know yet. I'll know when it is time, and I'll not only travel to the places he's called me, but I'll also travel to the places where I haven't been called yet, but will be.

That's how I'd encourage you. Take God at his word, as a lamp for your feet and a light for your path. There will be light for each step. He will walk the path with you. Enjoy the scenery along the way. Don't rush the process…it'll only slow you down.

Moments of Reflection

1. What dreams have you had that you know are directional for your walk?

2. Evaluate those dreams. Are they pointing toward the giver of the promise or the promise?

3. What are some promises God has made to you specifically that have already come to fruition? Have you thanked him for those?

4. What are some promises that haven't come to pass yet? Have you thanked him for those?

5. How is he currently lighting your own path?

Prayer of Refining

Dear Abba, I am your child. Just like an earthly father would teach us how to walk, I ask that you would teach me how to walk. Help me recognize each step as you light the path. God, you are so holy and so pure. I want my own life to reflect those facets of your character. When the path seems too long or unclear, help me to rest in your embrace until I can see clearly again.

In the name of Jesus, so be it. Amen!

Persevering in the Storm

After Deep Calls to Deep Ministries was formed, a lot of individual things shifted for me. In the development phase, one of the things I did was assemble a council of advisors. It was a small beginning, but from day one, we had said that we would remember that "he who is faithful in a very little thing is faithful also in much, and he who is unrighteous in a very little thing is unrighteous also in much" (Luke 16:10 NASB).

The first year, we were able to help sponsor a Christmas party for the children at my friend's ministry in India. For some time, the Lord had been speaking to me about the difference between meeting basic needs versus fulfilling hearts' desires. I noticed the abundance of scriptures about that very topic, abundance, and I began to understand how, for too long, we've focused more on only meeting basic needs. But God is into the concept of overflow. The more I thought about the kids at my friend's ministry, the more I realized that in addition to attending to their basic needs, what made her ministry special to me was the way she longed to minister to their hearts. So at some point, I asked her what we could do just to show love to them. The topic of a Christmas party came up, and it was a perfect fit for what I wanted to do for them.

While I wasn't there in person, I saw photos later, and my heart was overwhelmed. The smiles on those little faces were incredible. From that point forward,

I knew I wanted to continue to grow into a place of ministering to those deepest hearts' desires, to those children again as well as to whomever else God would call me and in whatever manner he'd call me.

However, at the same time the ministry was slowly growing and taking shape, my carefully balanced life at home was beginning to fall apart. While I am expecting a miracle, the facts of my life have been that I need help with what are called activities of daily living, or ADLs. These ADLs include bathing, dressing, going to the bathroom, doing my makeup, etc. Basically, every major life activity fits in that category. Throughout my life, for a variety of reasons, my parents had been my primary caregivers. Over the years though, my dad's health began to fail, and in December of 2008, he was diagnosed with Lewy body dementia. He had already faced a past heart attack, lung problems, a triple bypass heart surgery, and prostate cancer. This hit all of the family with a hard blow. I remember sitting in the neurologist's office with Daddy as the doctor told me he would forget how to do things, that he would remember people and past events, but he would forget processes, and that he would begin having problems with mobility. I rebuked that diagnosis and prayed for him to be healed. But for reasons beyond my human understanding, his condition progressed, and he had to take a lesser and lesser role in my care and in household activities.

Suddenly, we were a household of four, each with vastly different needs. I had physical care needs, my sister needed direction and some care, my dad was growing sicker by the day, and my mom was overwhelmed with the strain of caregiving and household upkeep. During all this time, we were still trying to function as if nothing was wrong. I was still working full time, going into all of Dad's appointments with him, volunteering, and nurturing this newborn ministry. My mom was doing all the typical household chores and all the caregiving, driving to the doctors sometimes twice and three times weekly, staying in the van with Sissy while I went in with Dad, and driving me to work. My dad was slowly slipping away from us, frustrated at himself for not being able to do what he once could, and becoming more childlike almost on a daily basis. My sister was confused, not able to comprehend why her Daddy wasn't the same anymore. My brother helped as much as he could, but he had his own family, a full-time job, and a farm to maintain. It just wasn't feasible for him to be there all the time. We were all exhausted.

I felt like giving up. The ministry had just begun, and already a spirit of heaviness hovered over it, ready to kill it before it could go any further. I prayed harder than I ever had for wisdom about what to do. Should I stop? Should I continue? I knew that God had opened the door in the first place, and I knew that it was counterintuitive to the concept of spreading the gospel to stop it. So I slowly kept moving forward. At times, the distractions were so unrelenting that I couldn't see through the fog. My only relief became something I'd later call "Abba time." I'd slip outside in the warm Georgia evenings to stroll around, just worshiping, and praying and trying to stay in a place of peace amidst the whirlwind. I'd cry out to God as my Abba Father, asking him to keep me and to sustain me and my entire family through the storm. It was out of those times with him that my first book was birthed and appropriately titled, "Abba Time."

It felt like everything was crashing around me. I had a million questions and no one had any more answers than I did. My family had lived in a precarious balance for years, particularly regarding care for all of us, and that balance had been disrupted. Now, I felt like I had lost my security, my stability, my dreams, and on top of it all, I was losing my dad. I won't lie…at times during those years, I went to the Lord, with a raw and bleeding heart, asking him why this was happening. I even struggled at times with no longer feeling his presence. Old wounds that I thought were healed and the anger I felt I had put behind me resurfaced.

One season was particularly hard. We had all reached a level where things could simply not remain the same. The stress level was atomic in intensity. I moved into a friend's house for three and a half months, where I learned how to live with help from caregivers other than my family. My brother and his family took Dad for a while until he could be placed in a nursing home where he could have 24/7 care. We were all torn apart, struggling to regain our footing.

During this time, I faced some of my own personal darkest fears. Even though I was a grown woman, I had always dreaded the day I'd need to rely on other people for help. Would anyone even be willing to help? Those old feelings of worthlessness threatened to drown me.

But still, somewhere inside me, there was that deep calling out to the deep. I had to come to a place of realizing something huge. When things change, *we change*. I kept moving forward, stepping out in faith, seeing God remain faithful to show me that he was the one with the master plan. I was a participant, but my life was still his plan. It was only three and a half months, but during that time, I felt like I was on a decades-long rollercoaster of emotion.

As that semester at work finished and as Christmas drew near, I was sitting in the quietness at my friend's house one day when I heard the Lord speak softly to my spirit.

"I want you to go home now."

It wasn't a command. It wasn't a question. It was simply him expressing his desire for my life, but I knew I had a choice. I had found comfort in discovering that independence was possible for me, but I also missed my family too. I knew my mom wanted me to come home, my sister missed me, and I also knew that my dad's time on earth was drawing to a close. What the Holy Spirit revealed to me was that if I truly believed in grace, this was an opportunity to show that I believed it. By going back home, I would be both giving and receiving grace.

So I went home. Prior to my leaving, the relationship between my mom and I had been severely strained. But I understood why. We were both beyond exhaustion. When I moved back home, we became much closer than we'd ever been. I had always wanted to have one of those mother/daughter relationships where the two are genuinely friends, and today, I have that. We still don't always agree, but we do value each other as individuals, and that's precious to me. It was a bumpy road, but the end result was worth it. I'm very grateful to have such a strong woman as my mother.

For the next few months, I focused on work and we visited Dad in the nursing home as often as we could. One day in March, my brother called to tell us that the home had called to tell him Dad had pneumonia, and that they were beginning treatment. We were all obviously concerned, but we were all also assured that the medication should clear things up. Exactly a week later though, we were informed that the follow-up chest X-rays showed he now had pneumonia in both lungs and was being transported to the hospital. The prognosis wasn't good. Every treatment they tried for the pneumonia resulted in episodes of congestive heart failure. Treatment for the congestive heart failure would require valve replacement surgery, and he wasn't a candidate for that. He was too weak. So reality set in. We were now in the last leg of walking Daddy home.

My dad holding me on a carousel in Cherokee, North Carolina.

Dad loved making me laugh, even as a baby.

I cried a lot. My dad had always been such a source of strength and security. Now, the man who had seemed invincible was finishing his race. I couldn't physically care for him, and I didn't know how else to help him but to sit there with him. On the day the doctor told us we had probably no more than three days, my dad was sitting in bed. He didn't hear those words, but I really think he knew it was time. He wasn't able to talk anymore, but he said a lot with his eyes. I was sitting by his bed at the hospital, and he was more alert than he had been for a while. He reached over and pulled my hand onto the bed beside him and just held it. He tinkered with my watch a little, and then again just held my hand. For a while, he just looked intently at me, as if memorizing my face. I tried to talk, and in my goofy manner, even tried to make him laugh. But he just smiled weakly. I hushed and just let him hold my hand. At one point, a tear trickled down his face and he squeezed my hand. He couldn't say a word by then, but I knew he was telling me good-bye. All I could whisper was, "Oh, Daddy…" through my own tears. Eventually, he let go of my hand and drifted to sleep. But I now knew what I could do for him. I could hold his hand, and from that moment on, my prayer was, "God, please let me be holding his hand as he comes home to you." I sat by his bed, holding his hand.

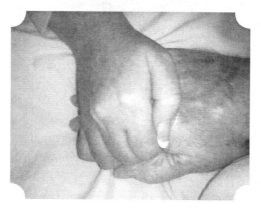

Daddy's hand in mine

Later that day, Monday, April 2, 2012, he was transferred back to the nursing home into the hospice room since there was nothing more the hospital could do for him. I continued to sit by him, holding his hand day and night, leaving only when the nurses and CNAs had to wash him or change his bedclothes. Mom and I only went home long enough for me to use the bathroom and freshen up, and for Mom to shower. The rest of our family stayed as much as they could too. On Thursday night, the CNAs came to change him again, and this time, I felt an urgency to stay. I couldn't leave. So I closed my eyes as they washed him again, and when they were done, I knew the time was near. I asked the nurses to please hurry and get the rest of the family back in the room. Within a couple of minutes, with us all around him, and yes, with me still holding his hand, he crossed the finish line. As a friend of mine, Carolyn, likes to say, "He exhaled his last time here, and immediately inhaled in heaven." In that moment, all I could do was pray, "God, thank you for his life."

After he passed, there was a renewed determination in me to introduce people to Jesus. The ministry didn't end…it was still only beginning. I've often told people since then that there's something indescribable about having someone that close to you now living in heaven. It's especially poignant when it's a blood relative. When we have the same DNA, there is literally a part of each relative in heaven and on earth simultaneously. In those last days with Dad, I had a chance to talk to him, sing to him, read the Bible to him, pray over him, and make promises to carry on his legacy of faith. He loved Jesus, and the Holy Spirit led me to talk to him about the story of the alabaster box in Matthew 26. In verse 13, Jesus said, "Truly I say to you, wherever this gospel is preached in the whole world, what this woman has done will also be spoken of in memory of her." I promised my dad that too…that like that woman, wherever I go, I will share that my dad was a tremendous man of integrity and faith in Christ and that my mother is a tremendous woman of strength and kingdom hospitality.

My dad and mom when I was very young.

Yes, obstacles and even disagreements will come. But the prize is always worth the process of perseverance. If there is something worth having, I've discovered that God is willing to give it freely, in the appropriate timing, but even in the appropriate timing, the enemy does want to abort it.

> Now may the God who gives perseverance and encouragement grant you to be of the same mind with one another according to Christ Jesus, so that with one accord you may with one voice glorify the God and Father of our Lord Jesus Christ.
>
> Romans 15: 5–6 (NASB)

Perseverance is a gift of grace from him, and is not obtained by our struggles. We are made stronger by the things in which we persevere, but perseverance itself is something he gives us. And when he gives us perseverance and encouragement, it leads to unity and the glorification of God.

Moments of Reflection

1. Have you ever started something only to feel like it is being stalled?

2. How did you respond in faith to those events?

3. How has he used those events to shape you?

4. Were those events actually hindrances after all?

5. How can you be prepared to recognize whether something is a hindrance or a divine detour?

Prayer of Refining

Dear Abba, in and of myself, I can do no good thing. But with Christ, all things are possible. You know my own limits and nothing surprises you. Lord, be my strength to persevere. I know your plans are incredible, so I want to cooperate fully with you. Hold me, and walk, and I will walk with you to the extent that I can. And beyond that, carry me. Empower me to finish all that you have begun in me. Thank you, Lord, for the grace it is impossible for me to earn.

In the name of Jesus, so be it. Amen!

Living Authentically

No testimony of my adventures thus far would be complete without sharing what it was like to grow up as a Cabbage Patch Kid. If anyone has any remembrance of pop culture during the 1980s in the United States, he or she will for sure remember the Cabbage Patch craze. Parents stood in and even got into brawls over these pudgy faced huggables when the phenomenon was at its height. And during all that, I was growing up in the patch. No, I didn't spring forth from a giant cabbage, but I was there watching it all happen from the beginning.

In 1978, the year after I was born, Xavier Roberts, a local man from my hometown, became what seemed to be an almost overnight celebrity for the dolls he envisioned and created in the style of folk art fabric sculptures. My family was, and still is, friends with his family, so I know that there was a much longer road involved in his success. To the outside world, it did indeed seem like Xavier was instantly famous. But the entire operation began very modestly, with the cloth from every doll being hand-cut with scissors into the patterned shapes needed to produce the bodies. It was slow-going growth, but it showed massive potential.

After a season of that slow progress, one of the most well-known women in our town, Dorothy Jean Payne, more commonly known simply as Dot, told Xavier that she knew a man who could cut out enough dolls in one weekend to supply the sewers and other artists for weeks. That man was my dad. He had worked in textiles most of his life, using a hand-operated cutting machine to cut clothing out for production. So Dot made that business connection, and from then on, I felt like I lived in the Cabbage Patch.

The original Babyland General Hospital, where the Cabbage Patch craze was "born."

Of course, in the earliest years, I was too young to remember a ton of specific details. However, some of my earliest memories were sitting in the basement of what later became known as Babyland General Hospital. As the phenomenon grew, the company eventually moved Dad's cutting operation into one of two small white cottages beside the "hospital." It had only three rooms and a tiny bathroom. One room was the cutting room, where the cutting table was and where all the work took place. The other two rooms stored huge rolls of fabric, stacked from floor to ceiling with a path just wide enough for my chair to roll through. We simply called it "the little house." My dad continued cutting out the dolls and clothes, and my mom was one of the women hired to work from home sewing yarn into curls on the doll heads. So on many nights after Dad left from his day job, he'd come home, and though Mom would have been sewing doll hair all day, she would've had supper ready, so we'd eat. Then we'd pile into our old station wagon and head to the little house, where Mom and Dad would work sometimes until one and two o'clock in the morning. During the peak of the fad, we were there on weekends from early morning until late night. When I'd get tired, I'd lay down to nap on blankets in the floor, with my head resting on stacks of cloth which would later become Cabbage Patch Kid bodies. Sitting in the cutting room is where I became a bookworm and where I spent so much time drawing. My folks were busy and my sister was too old to want to play with me, so I'd have a bag full of books, notebooks, pens, pencils, and toys packed to bring with me to keep myself occupied. I lived in my own little world, surrounded by the "magic" of the Cabbage Patch.

Things changed over the years, and eventually both my mom and dad stopped working for the factory, but during those years, I know from being there that there was literally sweat, blood, and tears involved. Sweat from their hard work, blood from run-ins with the cutting knife and staplers, and tears, probably mostly from me being whiny about being tired or bored!

It was a lot of behind-the-scenes work, but it was a very worthwhile part of our family's history. So "to everything there is a season" and my parents' season did eventually finish there. But it was a very long season, my entire childhood and into college. I have extremely fond memories of those days, and consider it a privilege to have been a part of one of the greatest toy stories of that decade, and perhaps in American history. In fact, even as a child, I did get to have one specific influence in the dolls' history. I remember one Saturday while the phenomenon was just getting off the ground, and I was sitting in the cutting room at the little house.

Since the products were expanding in popularity, in order to have baby dolls in a variety of skin colors for all children, a line of the first multicultural babies had been introduced in the full sized babies. The preemie line was just beginning to be more popular, so I asked if there were any black preemies yet, and Dad said there weren't, but he'd suggest it. And so he did and within weeks, I "adopted" (and still have) the first black preemie Cabbage Patch Kid. His name is Daniel Bruce. I also have one of the very first original full sized babies. For that one, the business was so new that the dolls didn't yet come with names and birth certificates, but I named her after myself. She was a gift to me from Xavier and like all the authentic originals, she has his signature on her rear.

This practice of him signing the dolls was actually what introduced me to the concept of authenticity. From a very early age, I knew how to tell the difference between the various knockoffs on the market and the real thing. I also knew the difference between the stamps on the rump and the handwritten signature. And I knew that it was the ones with the handwritten signatures that were the most valuable for collectors' purposes. This lesson learned from my years in the Cabbage Patch has really followed me throughout my life.

Over the years, I've come to appreciate authenticity more and more. I've realized things that look like the real thing sometimes aren't. And sometimes, even things that are the real thing are only stamped with an image of the authentic, rather than actually bearing "the signature." One thing that has really been deeply ingrained into me, especially since becoming Spirit-filled, is that I want to lead an authentic kingdom life, complete with every possible signature of God's identity handwritten in my life. I don't want to be a knockoff that is close-but-not-quite-the-real-thing. We've been warned in Scripture that there will be impostors.

> But realize this, that in the last days difficult times will come. For men will be lovers of self, lovers of money, boastful, arrogant, revilers, disobedient to parents, ungrateful, unholy, unloving, irreconcilable, malicious gossips, without self-control, brutal, haters of good, treacherous, reckless, conceited, lovers of pleasure rather than lovers of God, holding to a form of godliness, although they have denied its power; Avoid such men as these. For among them are those who enter into households and captivate weak women weighed down with sins, led on by various impulses, always learning and never able to come to the knowledge of the truth… Indeed, all who desire to live godly in

Christ Jesus will be persecuted. But evil men and impostors will proceed from bad to worse, deceiving and being deceived.

2 Timothy 3: 1–7, 12–13 (NASB)

And I don't even want to be just a lukewarm Christian with only the stamp of his name. His word makes clear how he views lukewarmness.

I know your deeds, that you are neither cold nor hot; I wish that you were cold or hot. So because you are lukewarm, and neither hot nor cold, I will spit you out of My mouth.

Revelation 3: 15–16 (NASB)

To bear only his name without the power it carries is not enough for me. I can't be content in being a poor attempt at a replica. I never want to be lukewarm. I want to be fully engulfed or not even lit. There is no middle ground for me, and I tend to want to do whatever I do with my full attention and at full acceleration. I remember sitting in a hotel lobby with Apostle Shirley and Pastor Loretta, spending some time talking until it was time for them to go back to the airport to leave. I was in the middle of explaining something and was talking about wanting to go full speed ahead with it. Apostle Shirley smiled and said, "You live your whole life like that, don't you?" My response was, "I have to… there is no other life for me."

I know I can never be Jesus, nor do I even remotely pretend to be. However, he *is* alive in me. His Spirit is at work in my life. I've made a ton of mistakes and

I've sinned, exceedingly so, and I'm fully aware of those mistakes and those sins, which are totally different things. However, by his *grace*, he chooses to "remember [them] no more" (Hebrews 8:12 NASB).

I can't change one thing I've ever done in my past. I can't go back and undo those things. But Jesus atoned for them, and when he did, he put his signature on me and my life. His name is written on me.

It doesn't mean that I will never do anything wrong again, because honestly, I'm still in a human body made of flesh. But it does mean that I now carry not only his name, but also the responsibilities of bringing honor to it and not dishonor. So it means that I will do everything I can to please him, not to win his love, because I already have that, but rather because I want to glorify his name. The best way I know to do so is to live authentically, sharing the ups and downs, the successes and failures, and all the hills and valleys in between. I wouldn't be honest if I said all things are perfect at all times. We live in a fallen world. But Jesus *is* perfect, and he *isn't* fallen, and in him, there is freedom to live authentically without fear that our weaknesses are stronger than his grace.

Moments of Reflection

1. Have you ever seen something that appeared to be "the real thing," only to later discover it wasn't?

2. What are the marks of his authenticity in your life?

3. How do they empower you to bear fruit?

4. How can you discern authenticity in circumstances?

5. Are there any areas of your life in which you know you want to live more authentically?

Prayer of Refining

Dear Abba, thank you for truth. The sacrifice of Jesus was as real and authentic as it gets. Let me never take that for granted. Thank you for the privilege of living authentically, with your seal upon me. I am not a carbon copy. I am not a cheap knockoff. I am a pearl of great price. Lord, show me how to live daily according to that authenticity. Make it so clear that when others encounter me, they encounter you.

In the name of Jesus, so be it. Amen!

Receiving Redemption

The older I've grown, the more "settled" I feel in my spirit. Call it growth, maturity, or whatever you'd like, but it's a really nice state of being. When I look back at my life, of course, I'm proud of the accomplishments from hard work. But I believe that even in my headstrong pridefulness, it was still God who opened those doors. So I would never say that hard work is a wrong or a bad thing. Even Jesus grew up as a carpenter's son, doing work. Furthermore, scriptures make it clear that we are involved in a real war, and we will assuredly face battles.

Yet what I've discovered is that it is not our efforts that determine the final outcome. It is what we allow God to do in and through us that determines the final outcome. As far as he is concerned, it is a finished race—a done deal. But there's still the "walking it out" we have to do. Even so, he is so faithful as a redeemer. So nowadays, even when the struggles come—and oh yes, they still come!—I find out that, sometimes even to my own surprise, I am at rest. Being surrendered to *his* plans is such an incredible place of power and peace. The real power comes when he is no longer our crutch, but our Redeemer. If I truly believe he is faithful, there's no longer a need to strive to figure things out. I must trust, and just let him be God in my life. I'm sure, to some, that sounds painfully cliché. But it is very true. He can take the most unusual or even difficult circumstances, and make lemonade out of those lemons. I don't know how he does it all, but I don't have to know. I'm just glad he is both sovereign and a redeemer. Interestingly, he has an incredible way of using our circumstances in spite of themselves to not only accomplish his purposes, but also to bring us joy in the process. That's one way to look at redemption. In fact, it is probably the most frequently looked at way to view the concept of redemption. But it isn't the only way. God has taught me something about redemption that has changed my own perspective, and I know that it can change yours too.

In recent years, here in the United States, giving gift cards has become quite popular. They're a convenient and still thoughtful way to give someone a gift that they will be sure to like. After all, if they can pick it out themselves, you can't go wrong as a giver, right? So, like anyone, I enjoy both giving and receiving gift cards. In and of themselves, they're just a piece of plastic, usually with a magnetic stripe on them. Some have pictures relevant to specific occasions, while some are more generic, and some are even customizable with the option to add your own images on them. But the basic premise is the same. Someone goes to a store, chooses a card, pays for a value to be attributed to it, and then gives it as a gift. The recipient then takes the card into the establishment for which it was intended, and redeems it for an item or items equal to that value.

I was sitting at home, thinking of a particular gift card. I am 100 percent certain that when it was given to me, the intent was not that I keep that little piece of plastic in my wallet forever. Instead, the intent was for me to redeem that card to obtain something I'd enjoy. I'd had my eyes on a particular item I'd wanted for a while, but I hadn't really had a reason to go buy it. But with this gift card to that establishment, I suddenly had a perfect reason to get what I had wanted. Mind you, us ladies realize that any reason is good enough. We need this scarf to match that sweater, or we need this bracelet to match that blouse, or we need this pair of shoes to match that skirt. Right? Well, I needed to use this gift card so I bought what I wanted and was really happy with it.

I'm sure that you may be wondering why this apparently materialistic anecdote fits in a chapter about redemption. But trust me, it does. It makes total sense, and here's what he taught me from the experience.

When Jesus came to earth to live, die, and be resurrected for our redemption, that once for all sacrifice was sufficient. His *blood* provided redemption for all, and he took on all sins. He bought it all. Sometimes people call it the great exchange. He paid for everything. And sometimes, we get so caught up in what he saved us *from* that we forget what he paid for that we are to receive. Yes, he died so we won't go to hell. But he resurrected so that we can reign in life now.

> But the free gift is not like the transgression. For if by the transgression of the one the many died, much more did the grace of God and the gift by the grace of the one Man, Jesus Christ, abound to the many. The gift is not like that which came through the one who sinned; for on the one hand the judgment arose from

> one transgression resulting in condemnation,
> but on the other hand the free gift arose from
> many transgressions resulting in justification.
> For if by the transgression of the one, death
> reigned through the one, much more those who
> receive the abundance of grace and of the gift
> of righteousness will reign in life through the
> One, Jesus Christ.
>
> Romans 5: 15–17 (NASB)

Something that I've often said is that it saddens me to see so many people still kneeling in the shadow underneath the empty cross. We should never, ever, *ever* disregard the tremendous sacrifice at the cross. We should never forget it. We should be grateful for it. But the cross is empty now. The cross Jesus died on has long since been taken down and destroyed. On the other hand, he is still very much alive. Therefore, when we receive the abundance of grace and of the gift of righteousness, we *will* reign in life through Jesus.

He gave us the ultimate gift card. We have all success at our fingertips. But it comes with a choice. Will we stay in the shadow of that empty cross where we received this gift card? Will we put it in a safe place and protect it, telling everyone about this fantastic gift card we received? Will we pull it out from time to time, looking at it, knowing the value of it, only to place it back in safekeeping? Or will we do what he intended for us to do with it? Will we redeem it for its full value, using it to receive the benefits of the gift?

Just as a gift card is just a piece of plastic with little monetary value when it isn't loaded, our lives seem meaningless without understanding them in the context of his value. However, a salvation experience can be compared to realizing that we're "loaded." We have value because he saved us and paid for us, so then we see what he's done. But then, we must be willing to go further, not just finally realizing our value, but actually using it. Just like it wasn't my friend's intent for me to stash that gift card forever, it also isn't God's intent for us to remain "purchased but unredeemed."

We are loaded with his benefits, and scripture encourages us not to forget them.

> Bless the Lord, O my soul: and all that is within me, bless his holy name.
>
> Bless the Lord, O my soul, and forget not all his benefits:
>
> Who forgiveth all thine iniquities; who healeth all thy diseases;
>
> Who redeemeth thy life from destruction; who crowneth thee with lovingkindness and tender mercies;
>
> Who satisfieth thy mouth with good things; so that thy youth is renewed like the eagle's.
>
> Psalm 103: 1–5 (KJV)

We are fully loaded, and ready to be redeemed. Now that Jesus has made the great exchange, we are to redeem his gift card by using all the value he's ascribed to us. We now get the joy of redeeming his purchase for a cause greater than ourselves, the advancement of his kingdom. We are redeemed to redeem—our receiving and walking out redemption leads to us redeeming the earth as well. Through Adam, Creation fell. Through Jesus, we were redeemed and are in the process of taking back what he purchased for us *and* for his purposes. He paid for it, now we have to go get it. This is where our unique giftings come in. They lead us into places of influence.

> A man's gift makes room for him and brings him before great men.
>
> Proverbs 18:16 (AMP)

When God gives us gifts, he will open doors for us to use them. However, ultimately it is up to us to use them. It's not his fault if we don't. He purchased them for us and gave them to us, but from then on, the ball is in our court. Just as a friend typically doesn't ask if you've redeemed the gift card he or she gave you, God, in his infinite grace, doesn't keep asking us over and over if we've redeemed it yet. He simply gives it and lets us choose whether we use it or keep it stashed away.

When I finally said yes to God, I didn't want to say yes only partially. I fell so in love with him that I didn't want to leave any part of his gift unused. It was like I suddenly awoke from a lifetime of slumber. I had known him before on a surface salvation level, but when I finally realized the safety in him leading my life through the Holy Spirit, it felt like I was a totally different person. I remember chatting with my friend Scott one night about this concept. We had been discussing the radical changes we'd both been through since becoming Spirit-baptized believers. I made the comment that it seemed like a lifetime ago. Scott's response was profoundly on target.

"It *was* a lifetime ago."

And it was. It was a confused, searching, unredeemed lifetime ago. But praise to Jesus, he changed all of that. I want to experience *all* of what he has for me. I cannot live all of my life with his gift hidden in my pocket. Instead, I want to spend it all for the sake of the kingdom.

Moments of Reflection

1. How has God redeemed certain things in your life?

2. What areas still need to be redeemed?

3. How can you submit those areas for redemption?

4. What are the gifts God has given you specifically?

5. How do you use them for the kingdom or how can you begin to do so if you haven't already?

Prayer of Refining

Dear Abba, you gave your most precious treasure, your son, to purchase freedom and abundant life for me. Without fail, you have remained faithful to the promises you provided through his sacrifice. Lord, I don't want to leave one single area of my life unredeemed. Show me how to live vibrantly, staying connected into your never-ending abundance at all times. Equip me to walk out this redemption for the purposes of advancing your kingdom.

In the name of Jesus, so be it. Amen!

Resting in Victory

These days, I'm more excited than ever about what is going on both in my own personal life as well as what is going on globally. I see events unfolding that biblical prophecy foretold thousands of years ago. A lot of people seem to be afraid, but I'm not. There's a deep passion for Jesus and for the things of the Holy Spirit in me. I ache to see miracles become the norm instead of the exception, and quite frankly, anything less is settling for status quo. We are not underdogs. It's time for the advancement forces in the kingdom of God to get out of the underdog mentality and start living as victorious ones. I want to see generations rise up to take their places in history. That kind of movement is birthed one life at a time. Each person must reach a place of confidence in identity that is so steadfast that nothing can sway them from the truth. And such a firm structure can only be built on one foundation.

> Nevertheless, the firm foundation of God stands, having this seal, "The Lord knows those who are His," and, "Everyone who names the name of the Lord is to abstain from wickedness."
>
> 2 Timothy 2:19 (NASB)

He is that foundation, and not only that, he bears the seal that declares he knows who we are. When we begin to walk in his identity for us, we must then make a conscious decision to commit to change. By his grace, we are made righteous, but by his mercy, we're given the liberty to grow in integrity as that righteousness fits more and more. He's already made the way, and usually, by the time we realize that fact, we're in need of a good cleanup job. I know for sure I was, and I know I've needed a repeat rinse more than once. I don't mean his sacrifice wasn't enough the first and only time, because it was. But what I mean is that if grace is like a waterfall, I've wandered into the desert more times than I would like to admit, and have had to make conscious decisions to trek back to and then to step back under that waterfall of grace. It flows only through Jesus…not through new age philosophy or positive thinking or any other religious icon. Grace flows only one way, through Jesus. He said, "I am the way and the truth and the life" (John 14: 6 NIV). He didn't say, "I am *a* way," nor did he say, "I am *one possible* way." He said, "I am *the* way." But in that one way, there is victory beyond description.

Victory is a journey.

Victory is not an objective to be reached. If we believe that, then we haven't yet grasped the fullness of the redemption. Instead, victory is a lifestyle. It's a journey. Since Jesus already obtained it for us and then gave it as a free gift, all we have to do is walk in it, to cash it in. We have the victory sufficient for overcoming all of the things we'll ever face.

> For whatever is born of God overcomes the world. And this is the victory that has overcome the world—our faith.
>
> 1 John 5:4 (NKJV)

Will we still face obstacles? Most assuredly so. On a daily basis, I am faced with the stark reality that my life would be so much easier if I could just walk, and even being able to scratch my own nose without help would be pretty cool. But for now, this is the set of circumstances I must operate within. Still, it doesn't discourage me. It has no power over my identity. He is *still* God and I am *still* his daughter. He continually amazes me with his faithfulness. Yes, it's still a fight, but I'm enjoying life and tremendously so, as a matter of fact. Nothing can tear me from his hand. I've learned that we must all remember that we do not fight for victory. Instead, we fight from inside a place of victory.

I don't know exactly when I will walk. I don't know the date when each promise he has given me will manifest. But I don't have to know. What I *do* know is that he is far greater than anything I can imagine, so I'm content in the waiting. While I wait, I see all kinds of opportunities. I relish all kinds of adventures, be they large or small. I am genuinely joyful, because his plans are trustworthy.

He has revolutionized my life by taking the ashes of what might've been and turning them into something incredible. It's not me...not my efforts or anything of any particular strength. Instead, it's what he has done and is still doing and will do. I haven't always understood things, but the more I surrender to him, the less understanding events and things matters. I was scheduled to die decades ago, but he didn't listen to diagnoses. I thought I was smart and intelligent, but he's used me most in the areas where I felt the most foolish. It's been a challenge to travel even out of state at times, but he's given me a heart for the nations. It's kind of funny actually. So I just keep saying yes because honestly, it's a fun ride...this thing called life. His surprises make me laugh because they're so thrilling.

Abba's surprises are the best.

If there's one thing I want to leave with you, it is this. *You are treasured by the Father of all Creation and*

Jesus is the way to receive his affections for you. No matter what you have or haven't done, He loves you with a radical love and extends to you a grace that almost seems scandalous because it is so vast. He wants to reveal to you all the amazing plans he has in store for you if you will trust him with your heart and commit to his ways and allow his Word to transform you. St. Catherine of Siena once said, "Be who God meant you to be and you will set the world on fire." If you say yes to Jesus and receive the Holy Spirit, I guarantee that you will find that the Father's plan for you is beyond your own wildest dreams. I can boldly, confidently, and yes, fierily promise you that you will be absolutely amazed at what he does in your life, both for you and through you. You were born to change the world. Will you say yes?

Moments of Reflection

1. Take some time to reflect on the victories in your life. List them. What pattern do you see?

2. Do you have to *feel* victorious to *be* victorious?

3. What and who make you victorious?

4. How does this encourage you to move forward?

5. Are you ready to set the world on fire for the kingdom of God?

Prayer of Refining

Dear Abba, if I could only ever pray just one prayer, may it always be thank you. Thank you for Jesus, for the cross, for the resurrection, and for your Holy Spirit. You are my joy, my redeemer, my Savior, my friend, my matchless king, my audience of one. God, I want nothing less than to surrender my entire life for your purposes. Wherever you take me, I am humbled and honored to serve. Lead me in victory, Lord. I am yours.

In the name of Jesus, so be it. Amen!